Echoes of Ancient Persia: Tales from a Timeless Land

"Within the tapestry of time, where sands of history meet the constellations of destiny, lies the heart of ancient Persia—a realm of stories woven by sages and dreamers, where the echoes of valour, wisdom, and wonder continue to resonate. As the pages of antiquity turn, may these tales remind us that the threads of human experience are timeless, and the spirit of the past lives on in the stories we share."

Dedicated to the people of Persia.

Journey through the Heart of Mystical Narratives

In the heart of ancient Persia, a realm steeped in history, culture, and the enchanting tapestry of myths, a treasure trove of narratives awaits. These stories, woven like intricate carpets, reveal the spirit of a civilization that once flourished beneath the embrace of the sun and the watchful gaze of the stars. With each tale, we are transported to a time where heroes and heroines walked among us, where wisdom flowed like rivers, and where the very earth seemed to resonate with the echoes of an era long past.

From the bustling bazaars of ancient cities to the tranquil gardens where philosophers pondered the mysteries of the cosmos, each story paints a vivid tableau of a bygone era. We encounter brave warriors whose valour was matched only by their honour, cunning sages whose insights ignited the fires of knowledge, and artisans whose creations breathed life into the sublime beauty of the world around them.

Through these tales, we witness the power of unity and diversity, as cultures intermingle like threads in a splendid tapestry. We delve into the spiritual realms where mystics whispered secrets to the wind, and navigate the labyrinthine alleys where destiny and choice converged. As the sun sets over the horizon, we embark on a journey—a journey through the timeless stories of ancient Persia. These narratives, meticulously crafted to resonate with the essence of a civilization that shaped the course of history, invite us to explore the threads of courage, wisdom, love, and the ineffable mysteries that bound the people of that land together.

Join us as we step into a world where the past comes alive, and where the echoes of ancient Persia continue to ripple through time, inspiring and enchanting those who listen to their whispers.

Welcome to **"Echoes of Ancient Persia: Tales from a Timeless Land."**

The Labyrinth of Wisdom

Lost and Found in the Sands of Time

In the heart of the bustling city of Perseopolis, where the aroma of spices filled the air and the grand bazaars overflowed with treasures, lived a young merchant named Cyrus. Cyrus's eyes held the reflections of distant horizons, and his heart resonated with the mysteries of the cosmos.

One day, as Cyrus was browsing the stalls of the bazaar, an old traveller with a staff adorned with shimmering crystals approached him. The traveller's eyes held the wisdom of the ages, and his presence seemed to carry the secrets of the universe. He observed Cyrus's trade with a knowing smile and said, "Your hands possess the skill to trade goods, but to truly understand the essence of prosperity, you must journey to the Labyrinth of Wisdom."

Intrigued by the traveller's words, Cyrus expressed his interest in undertaking the journey. The traveller nodded and handed him a small amulet adorned with symbols of constellations. "Carry this Amulet of Guidance with you, and let it light your path," he said. "Seek the Labyrinth of Wisdom, where the paths of knowledge and fate intertwine."

With the Amulet of Guidance in his hand and a heart brimming with curiosity, Cyrus set out on his journey to find the Labyrinth of Wisdom—a place spoken of in ancient tales, said to be a sanctuary where seekers of truth were not just travellers, but explorers of destiny. Guided by the stars and the echoes of forgotten whispers, he journeyed through deserts, crossed mountains, and embraced the mysteries and revelations that his path held.

One night, as the moon cast a silver glow over the sands and the stars sparkled like diamonds in the sky, Cyrus arrived at the entrance of the Labyrinth of Wisdom. The air was hushed, yet electric with an enigmatic energy. He noticed the labyrinth's archways, adorned with intricate patterns that seemed to shimmer with the dance of celestial bodies.

As Cyrus stepped into the labyrinth's twisting paths, he found himself enveloped in a soft luminescence—a glow that seemed to come from the very stones themselves. He held up the Amulet of Guidance, and as its constellations aligned with the stars above, the labyrinth's passages began to shift and reconfigure in response.

With a sense of wonder, Cyrus moved deeper into the labyrinth. He navigated its turns, encountering symbols and riddles that seemed to test his understanding of the universe.
Each step was a journey within, and each puzzle he solved revealed a new layer of insight—a revelation that transcended the boundaries of knowledge and belief.

With the Amulet of Guidance in his hand, Cyrus reached the heart of the labyrinth—an open chamber where a celestial map was etched onto the floor. He gazed at the map, his eyes tracing the patterns of stars and planets, and suddenly, a realisation struck him. The map was not just a representation of the cosmos; it was a reflection of the journey he had undertaken, a testament to the interplay of destiny and choice.

As dawn broke and painted the horizon with hues of gold and rose, Cyrus's contemplation gradually subsided, leaving him standing in the chamber bathed in a soft, ethereal light. He knew that the Labyrinth of Wisdom had granted him a gift—the realisation that prosperity was not just material gain, but the alignment of one's path with the universal currents of existence.

With the Amulet of Guidance in his hand and a spirit illuminated by the essence of wisdom, Cyrus returned to Perseopolis. He shared the tale of the "Labyrinth of Wisdom" and the revelations he had experienced with his fellow merchants and dreamers, reminding them that the connection between trade and destiny was a dance of understanding and awareness, and that the pursuit of prosperity was a symphony of alignment and insight.

And so, dear listener, the story of Cyrus and the "Labyrinth of Wisdom" teaches us that prosperity is a journey that transcends material wealth, that the connection between trader and fate is a dance of consciousness and synchronicity, and that the essence of wisdom is a timeless truth from the heart of ancient Persia.

The Starlit Confluence

When Destinies Align in the Celestial Dance

In a village nestled at the edge of a tranquil oasis, where date palms rustled in the breeze and the soothing murmur of water kissed the air, lived a young astronomer named Leyla. Leyla's eyes held the wonder of the cosmos, and her heart resonated with the mysteries of the stars.

One evening, as Leyla was perched atop her observatory, charting the constellations that adorned the night sky, an old sage with a staff adorned with sparkling gems approached her. The sage's eyes held the depth of the heavens, and his presence seemed to carry the whispers of celestial secrets. He observed Leyla's observations with a knowing smile and said, "Your eyes possess the vision to perceive the cosmos, but to truly understand the essence of connection, you must journey to the Starlit Confluence."

Intrigued by the sage's words, Leyla expressed her interest in undertaking the journey. The sage nodded and handed her a small astrolabe adorned with intricate patterns. "Carry this Astrolabe of Alignment with you, and let it guide your path," he said. "Seek the Starlit Confluence, where the threads of fate converge under the watchful eyes of the stars."

With the Astrolabe of Alignment in her hand and a heart brimming with curiosity, Leyla set out on her journey to find the Starlit Confluence—a place whispered about in ancient tales, said to be a sanctuary where seekers of destiny were not just stargazers, but participants in the cosmic symphony.
Guided by the constellations and the melodies of the night, she journeyed through valleys, crossed deserts, and embraced the mysteries and revelations that her path held.

One night, as the moon cast its silvery glow over the landscape and the stars shimmered like diamonds on velvet, Leyla arrived at the Starlit Confluence. The air was still, yet vibrant with an otherworldly energy. She noticed the confluence's pathways, adorned with luminous stones that seemed to echo the patterns of the skies.

As Leyla walked along the paths of the confluence, she found herself surrounded by an iridescent luminescence—a light that seemed to come from both above and below. She held up the Astrolabe of

Alignment, and as its patterns resonated with the stars, the confluence's glow intensified, creating a celestial dance of light and shadow.

With a sense of awe, Leyla followed the pathways deeper into the confluence. She passed by markers that represented significant celestial events and dates, and as she moved among them, she felt a connection—a sensation that transcended time and space. The astrolabe in her hand seemed to be attuned to the rhythms of the universe itself.

With the Astrolabe of Alignment in her hand, Leyla reached the centre of the confluence—a circular space where the patterns of the heavens were recreated in intricate mosaics. She gazed at the mosaic, her eyes tracing the lines and symbols that echoed the constellations above. Suddenly, a realisation dawned upon her. The mosaic was not just a reflection of the stars; it was a representation of the interconnectedness of all things.

As dawn broke and painted the horizon with hues of gold and orange, Leyla's contemplation gradually came to an end, leaving her standing in the centre of the confluence bathed in a soft, ethereal light. She knew that the Starlit Confluence had granted her a gift—the realisation that destiny was not just written in the stars, but a confluence of choices and connections that flowed through every life.

With the Astrolabe of Alignment in her hand and a spirit illuminated by the essence of connection, Leyla returned to her village. She shared the tale of the "Starlit Confluence" and the revelations she had experienced with her fellow astronomers and dreamers, reminding them that the bond between observer and observed was a dance of interplay and unity, and that the pursuit of understanding the cosmos was a symphony of alignment and awareness.

And so, dear listener, the story of Leyla and the "Starlit Confluence" teaches us that connection is a journey that transcends the boundaries of space, that the bond between seeker and stars is a dance of participation and resonance, and that the essence of destiny is a timeless truth from the heart of ancient Persia.

The Weaver's Legacy

Threads of Fate Unraveled and Rewoven

In a village nestled at the foothills of the Zagros Mountains, where the scent of wildflowers mingled with the crisp mountain air and the echo of distant waterfalls filled the valley, lived a young weaver named Farah. Farah's eyes held the colours of the earth, and her heart resonated with the rhythms of creation.

One day, as Farah was carefully threading her loom with threads of wool and silk, an old storyteller with a staff adorned with intricate carvings approached her. The storyteller's eyes held the knowledge of ages past, and his presence seemed to carry the echoes of countless tales. He observed Farah's weaving with a knowing smile and said, "Your hands possess the skill to weave stories into fabric, but to truly understand the essence of stories, you must journey to the Spindle of Legends."

Intrigued by the storyteller's words, Farah expressed her interest in undertaking the journey. The storyteller nodded and handed her a small spindle adorned with ancient symbols. "Carry this Spindle of Legends with you, and let it guide your path," he said. "Seek the Spindle of Legends, where the threads of history and imagination intertwine."

With the Spindle of Legends in her hand and a heart brimming with curiosity, Farah set out on her journey to find the Spindle of Legends—a place spoken of in ancient tales, said to be a sanctuary where the art of storytelling was not just a craft, but a tapestry of cultural heritage and imagination. Guided by the stars and the whispers of the wind, she journeyed through forests, crossed rivers, and embraced the mysteries and revelations that her path held.

One evening, as the sun dipped below the horizon and the stars began to twinkle like stories in the sky, Farah arrived at the entrance of the Spindle of Legends. The air was alive with a sense of wonder, and she noticed the spindle's entrance, adorned with intricate carvings that seemed to come to life in the flickering torchlight.

As Farah stepped into the spindle's central chamber, she found herself surrounded by the soft glow of lanterns—a gentle illumination that seemed to beckon her to explore. She held up the Spindle of Legends, and as its symbols caught the light, the chamber's atmosphere seemed to shift and shimmer, as if welcoming her into the world of stories.

With a sense of anticipation, Farah moved deeper into the chamber. She walked past tapestries, scrolls, and tomes of every kind, each one a testament to the power of storytelling. As she moved among the stories, she felt a connection—an interweaving of emotions and experiences that transcended individual tales.

With the Spindle of Legends in her hand, Farah found herself before a mural that depicted a grand epic—a story that spanned generations, cultures, and landscapes.

As she gazed at the mural, she closed her eyes and allowed her imagination to merge with the narrative. She felt a shift in the chamber's energy—the rustling leaves, the laughter of characters, and the echoes of adventures all seemed to converge into a symphony of narratives.

As dawn broke and painted the horizon with hues of pink and gold, Farah's meditation gradually came to an end, leaving her standing in the chamber bathed in a soft, ethereal light. She knew that the Spindle of Legends had granted her a gift—the realisation that stories were not just words on a page, but the threads of cultural heritage and shared experiences that bound humanity together.

With the Spindle of Legends in her hand and a spirit illuminated by the essence of storytelling, Farah returned to her village. She shared the tale of the "Spindle of Legends" and the revelations she had experienced with her fellow weavers and dreamers, reminding them that the connection between weaver and tale was a dance of interpretation and imagination, and that the art of storytelling was a symphony of heritage and inspiration.

And so, dear listener, the story of Farah and the "Spindle of Legends" teaches us that storytelling is a journey that transcends time and culture, that the connection between weaver and narrative is a dance of interpretation and imagination, and that the essence of cultural heritage is a timeless truth from the heart of ancient Persia.

The Alchemist's Quest

Seeking Transmutation of Self and World

In a city of bustling markets and ornate palaces, where the aroma of spices hung in the air and the echoes of commerce filled the streets, lived a young alchemist named Zayd. Zayd's eyes held the glimmer of secrets yet uncovered, and his heart resonated with the mysteries of transformation.

One day, as Zayd was carefully measuring and mixing his elixirs in his workshop, an old sage with a staff adorned with alchemical symbols approached him. The sage's eyes held the depth of hidden knowledge, and his presence seemed to carry the echoes of ancient formulas. He observed Zayd's work with a knowing smile and said, "Your hands possess the skill to transmute elements, but to truly understand the essence of alchemy, you must journey to the Source of Unity."

Intrigued by the sage's words, Zayd expressed his interest in undertaking the journey. The sage nodded and handed him a small flask adorned with intricate patterns. "Carry this Flask of Harmony with you, and let it guide your path," he said. "Seek the Source of Unity, where the elements of self and world merge."

With the Flask of Harmony in his hand and a heart brimming with curiosity, Zayd set out on his journey to find the Source of Unity—a place spoken of in enigmatic whispers, said to be a sanctuary where alchemists were not just seekers of transmutation, but seekers of the interconnectedness of all things. Guided by the constellations and the echoes of ancient wisdom, he journeyed through deserts, crossed rivers, and embraced the mysteries and revelations that his path held.

One night, as the moon cast a silvery glow over the landscape and the stars shimmered like precious stones in the sky, Zayd arrived at the entrance of the Source of Unity. The air was still, yet charged with an ethereal energy. He noticed the source's entrance, adorned with geometric patterns that seemed to ripple like water.

As Zayd stepped into the source's inner chamber, he found himself surrounded by a gentle luminosity—an illumination that seemed to emanate from the very walls. He held up the Flask of Harmony, and as its patterns caught the light, the chamber's atmosphere began to shift and morph, as if inviting him to explore its depths.

With a sense of wonder, Zayd moved deeper into the chamber. He walked past crystals, vessels, and symbols of alchemical transformation, each one a testament to the mysteries of the craft. As he moved among the symbols, he felt a connection—an interplay of elements that transcended the boundaries of substances.

With the Flask of Harmony in his hand, Zayd approached a pool of shimmering liquid—the very essence of the Source of Unity. He gazed at his reflection in the liquid and closed his eyes, allowing his thoughts to merge with the patterns of the liquid's surface. He felt a shift in the chamber's energy—the rippling patterns, the hum of cosmic vibrations, and the whispers of ages all seemed to harmonise into a symphony of interconnectedness.

As dawn broke and painted the horizon with hues of orange and gold, Zayd's meditation gradually came to an end, leaving him standing by the pool bathed in a soft, ethereal light. He knew that the Source of Unity had granted him a gift—the realisation that alchemy was not just the transmutation of elements, but the understanding of the profound unity that underlies all creation.

With the Flask of Harmony in his hand and a spirit illuminated by the essence of interconnectedness, Zayd returned to his city. He shared the tale of the "Source of Unity" and the revelations he had experienced with his fellow alchemists and seekers, reminding them that the bond between elements and the self was a dance of unity and transformation, and that the pursuit of alchemy was a symphony of harmony and enlightenment.

And so, dear listener, the story of Zayd and the "Source of Unity" teaches us that alchemy is a journey that transcends the mere manipulation of substances, that the connection between alchemist and creation is a dance of understanding and unity, and that the essence of transformation is a timeless truth from the heart of ancient Persia.

The Oracle's Song

Echoes of Prophecy and Destiny

In a hidden valley, where ancient trees whispered secrets to the wind and the waters of a sacred spring danced in the sunlight, lived a young oracle named Darius. Darius's eyes held the depth of visions, and his heart resonated with the rhythms of the unseen.

One day, as Darius was sitting by the spring, his mind lost in contemplation, an old mystic with a staff adorned with crystals approached him. The mystic's eyes held the wisdom of ages beyond, and his presence seemed to carry the echoes of distant futures. He observed Darius's meditations with a knowing smile and said, "Your thoughts possess the power to unveil destinies, but to truly understand the essence of prophecy, you must journey to the Echoing Pool."

Intrigued by the mystic's words, Darius expressed his interest in undertaking the journey. The mystic nodded and handed him a small mirror adorned with intricate engravings. "Carry this Mirror of Reflection with you, and let it guide your path," he said. "Seek the Echoing Pool, where the songs of prophecy and the whispers of fate intertwine."

With the Mirror of Reflection in his hand and a heart brimming with curiosity, Darius set out on his journey to find the Echoing Pool—a place whispered about in enigmatic tales, said to be a sanctuary where seers were not just interpreters of visions, but participants in the cosmic narrative. Guided by the stars and the rustling of ancient leaves, he journeyed through forests, crossed rivers, and embraced the mysteries and revelations that his path held.

One night, as the moon bathed the landscape in a gentle glow and the stars sparkled like gems in the heavens, Darius arrived at the entrance of the Echoing Pool. The air was hushed, yet alive with an otherworldly energy. He noticed the pool's entrance, adorned with intricate engravings that seemed to come alive in the moonlight.

As Darius stepped into the pool's central clearing, he found himself surrounded by a soft radiance—a glow that seemed to emanate from the very earth. He held up the Mirror of Reflection, and as its engravings caught the moon's light, the pool's surface began to shimmer and ripple, like an ever-changing canvas of visions.

With a sense of anticipation, Darius moved closer to the pool. He gazed into the water's depths and saw images—fragments of events, faces of individuals, and landscapes that seemed to blur the lines between past, present, and future. Each reflection held a story—a piece of the cosmic puzzle.

With the Mirror of Reflection in his hand, Darius knelt by the pool's edge and touched the water's surface with his fingers. As his touch connected with the water, the images seemed to come alive, merging and converging into a symphony of sights and sounds—a tapestry of prophecies and echoes.

With closed eyes and a heart open to the currents of destiny, Darius listened to the echoes of the pool—the voices of seers, the laughter of ancestors, and the whispers of tales yet untold. He felt a shift in the pool's energy—the ripples, the melodies, and the harmonies all seemed to synchronise into a chorus of interconnected narratives.

As dawn broke and painted the sky with hues of pink and gold, Darius's meditation gradually came to an end, leaving him sitting by the pool bathed in a soft, ethereal light. He knew that the Echoing Pool had granted him a gift—the realisation that prophecy was not just a glimpse into the future, but a reflection of the interwoven stories that shaped the world.

With the Mirror of Reflection in his hand and a spirit illuminated by the essence of prophecy, Darius returned to his valley. He shared the tale of the "Echoing Pool" and the revelations he had experienced with his fellow seers and dreamers, reminding them that the connection between seer and vision was a dance of interpretation and insight, and that the pursuit of prophecy was a symphony of understanding and interconnectedness.

And so, dear listener, the story of Darius and the "Echoing Pool" teaches us that prophecy is a journey that transcends time and perception, that the bond between seer and vision is a dance of interpretation and insight, and that the essence of fate is a timeless truth from the heart of ancient Persia.

The Weaver of Dreams

Threads of Imagination Woven into Reality

In a quiet village nestled at the edge of a shimmering oasis, where date palms swayed to the rhythm of the wind and the song of the river echoed in the air, lived a young dreamweaver named Layla. Layla's eyes held the sparkle of unexplored realms, and her heart resonated with the melodies of the unseen.

One day, as Layla was sketching intricate patterns in the sand, an old sage with a staff adorned with ethereal feathers approached her. The sage's eyes held the light of distant worlds, and his presence seemed to carry the echoes of forgotten dreams. He observed Layla's creations with a knowing smile and said, "Your hands possess the skill to weave dreams into existence, but to truly understand the essence of creation, you must journey to the Weaver's Nexus."

Intrigued by the sage's words, Layla expressed her interest in undertaking the journey. The sage nodded and handed her a small loom adorned with delicate symbols. "Carry this Loom of Imagination with you, and let it guide your path," he said. "Seek the Weaver's Nexus, where the threads of dreams and reality entwine."

With the Loom of Imagination in her hand and a heart brimming with curiosity, Layla set out on her journey to find the Weaver's Nexus—a place whispered about in enigmatic tales, said to be a sanctuary where dreamweavers were not just creators of illusions, but co-creators of the world. Guided by the constellations and the whispers of the river, she journeyed through valleys, crossed meadows, and embraced the mysteries and revelations that her path held.

One night, as the moon cast its silvery glow over the landscape and the stars shimmered like fragments of forgotten dreams, Layla arrived at the entrance of the Weaver's Nexus. The air was hushed, yet alive with a sense of enchantment. She noticed the nexus's entrance, adorned with patterns that seemed to dance and shift with her gaze.

As Layla stepped into the nexus's central chamber, she found herself surrounded by a soft luminescence—a glow that seemed to come from the very air itself. She held up the Loom of Imagination, and as its symbols caught the light, the nexus's atmosphere began to transform, as if inviting her to weave her own reality.

With a sense of wonder, Layla moved deeper into the chamber. She walked past mirrors, tapestries, and doorways that led to unexplored horizons, each one a testament to the boundless possibilities of creation. As she moved among the symbols, she felt a connection—an interplay of dreams and existence that transcended the boundaries of perception.

With the Loom of Imagination in her hand, Layla approached a shimmering pool—the very heart of the Weaver's Nexus. She gazed into the pool and allowed her thoughts to merge with the ripples of its surface. She felt a shift in the nexus's energy—the shimmering lights, the whispers of potential, and the echoes of unspoken desires all seemed to harmonize into a symphony of co-creation.

With eyes closed and heart open to the canvas of reality, Layla began to weave—using the symbols of the Loom of Imagination to craft her dreams into existence. She watched as the threads of her intent intertwined, forming patterns that glimmered with the essence of possibility. The pool's surface seemed to mirror her visions, reflecting back the worlds she wove.

As dawn broke and painted the sky with hues of gold and rose, Layla's weaving gradually came to an end, leaving her standing by the pool bathed in a soft, ethereal light. She knew that the Weaver's Nexus had granted her a gift—the realisation that creation was not just an act of making, but a dance of intention and imagination.

With the Loom of Imagination in her hand and a spirit illuminated by the essence of creation, Layla returned to her village. She shared the tale of the "Weaver's Nexus" and the revelations she had experienced with her fellow dreamweavers and visionaries, reminding them that the connection between dream and reality was a dance of intention and inspiration, and that the pursuit of creation was a symphony of imagination and co-creation.

And so, dear listener, the story of Layla and the "Weaver's Nexus" teaches us that creation is a journey that transcends the mere act of making, that the bond between dreamer and reality is a dance of intention and imagination, and that the essence of possibility is a timeless truth from the heart of ancient Persia.

The Enchanted Minstrel

Melodies that Shape the Tapestry of Life

In a city of opulent palaces and bustling markets, where the fragrance of exotic spices wafted through the air and the symphony of voices echoed through the narrow streets, lived a young minstrel named Azar. Azar's eyes held the spark of inspiration, and his heart resonated with the harmonies of the universe.

One day, as Azar was playing his lute in a crowded square, an old bard with a staff adorned with vibrant ribbons approached him. The bard's eyes held the wisdom of countless stories, and his presence seemed to carry the echoes of ancient melodies. He observed Azar's performance with a knowing smile and said, "Your music possesses the power to stir emotions, but to truly understand the essence of harmony, you must journey to the Songbird's Refuge."

Intrigued by the bard's words, Azar expressed his interest in undertaking the journey. The bard nodded and handed him a small flute adorned with intricate carvings. "Carry this Flute of Echoes with you, and let it guide your path," he said. "Seek the Songbird's Refuge, where the melodies of creation and the rhythms of existence intertwine."

With the Flute of Echoes in his hand and a heart brimming with curiosity, Azar set out on his journey to find the Songbird's Refuge—a place spoken of in tales, said to be a sanctuary where minstrels were not just performers, but co-creators of reality through their melodies. Guided by the constellations and the whispers of the wind, he journeyed through valleys, crossed bridges, and embraced the mysteries and revelations that his path held.

One evening, as the sun dipped below the horizon and the stars emerged in the velvety sky, Azar arrived at the entrance of the Songbird's Refuge. The air was alive with the delicate flutter of wings and the gentle rustling of leaves. He noticed the refuge's entrance, adorned with carvings that seemed to depict nature and music intertwining.

As Azar stepped into the refuge's heart, he found himself surrounded by an ethereal aura—a glow that seemed to emanate from every blade of grass and every leaf on the trees. He held up the Flute of Echoes, and as its carvings caught the light, the refuge's atmosphere shifted, becoming a living canvas where melodies seemed to dance in the air.

With a sense of wonder, Azar moved deeper into the refuge. He walked among the trees, through gardens of blooming flowers, and beside streams that seemed to hum a symphony of their own.
As he moved among the melodies, he felt a connection—an interplay of sounds and sensations that transcended the boundaries of sound.

With the Flute of Echoes in his hand, Azar came upon a natural amphitheatre—a circular clearing where the very essence of the Songbird's Refuge seemed to converge. He gazed at the amphitheatre and closed his eyes, allowing his thoughts to merge with the rhythms of his surroundings. He felt a shift in the refuge's energy—the melodies, the rustling leaves, and the distant echoes all seemed to harmonise into a symphony of interconnected life.

With eyes closed and heart attuned to the pulse of existence, Azar lifted the Flute of Echoes to his lips and began to play. The notes that emerged were not just music—they were threads woven into the tapestry of reality itself. Each tone resonated with the world around him, amplifying the beauty of nature and evoking emotions that mirrored the landscape.

As dawn broke and painted the horizon with hues of orange and gold, Azar's playing gradually came to an end, leaving him standing in the amphitheatre bathed in a soft, ethereal light. He knew that the Songbird's Refuge had granted him a gift—the realisation that music was not just an art form, but a language that allowed one to co-create with the universe.

With the Flute of Echoes in his hand and a spirit illuminated by the essence of harmony, Azar returned to his city. He shared the tale of the "Songbird's Refuge" and the revelations he had experienced with his fellow musicians and dreamers, reminding them that the connection between minstrel and melody was a dance of co-creation and resonance, and that the pursuit of harmony was a symphony of unity and expression.

And so, dear listener, the story of Azar and the "Songbird's Refuge" teaches us that music is a journey that transcends mere performance, that the bond between musician and melody is a dance of co-creation and resonance, and that the essence of harmony is a timeless truth from the heart of ancient Persia.

The Garden of Whispers

Where Nature Holds Secrets and Stories

In a remote village nestled at the foothills of towering mountains, where the scent of wildflowers mingled with the crisp breeze and the songs of birds echoed through the valleys, lived a young herbalist named Soroush. Soroush's eyes held the wisdom of the earth, and his heart resonated with the mysteries of nature.

One day, as Soroush was tending to his garden, an old sage with a staff adorned with feathers approached him. The sage's eyes held the light of ancient knowledge, and his presence seemed to carry the echoes of forgotten stories. He observed Soroush's work with a knowing smile and said, "Your hands possess the skill to nurture life, but to truly understand the essence of nature, you must journey to the Grove of Whispers."

Intrigued by the sage's words, Soroush expressed his interest in undertaking the journey. The sage nodded and handed him a small vial adorned with intricate carvings. "Carry this Vial of Tranquility with you, and let it guide your path," he said. "Seek the Grove of Whispers, where the secrets of the earth and the stories of the wind intertwine."

With the Vial of Tranquility in his hand and a heart brimming with curiosity, Soroush set out on his journey to find the Grove of Whispers—a place whispered about in tales, said to be a sanctuary where herbalists were not just healers, but listeners to the voices of the natural world. Guided by the constellations and the rustling leaves, he journeyed through forests, climbed hills, and embraced the mysteries and revelations that his path held.

One evening, as the sun dipped below the horizon and the stars emerged like gems in the twilight sky, Soroush arrived at the entrance of the Grove of Whispers. The air was alive with the rustling of leaves and the gentle susurrus of unseen creatures. He noticed the grove's entrance, adorned with symbols that seemed to dance in the fading light.

As Soroush stepped into the grove's heart, he found himself surrounded by a soft luminescence—an aura that seemed to emanate from every blade of grass and every petal of a flower. He held up the Vial of Tranquility, and as its carvings caught the fading light, the grove's atmosphere transformed, becoming a haven where nature's voices seemed to harmonise.

With a sense of reverence, Soroush moved deeper into the grove. He walked among the trees, touched the petals of blooming flowers, and felt the earth beneath his feet. As he moved among the plants, he felt a connection—an interplay of energies that transcended the boundaries of human perception.

With the Vial of Tranquility in his hand, Soroush found himself before a natural amphitheatre—a circular clearing where the very essence of the Grove of Whispers seemed to converge. He gazed at the amphitheatre and closed his eyes, allowing his senses to merge with the symphony of nature's voices. He felt a shift in the grove's energy—the rustling leaves, the flowing waters, and the echoes of creatures all seemed to harmonise into a chorus of interconnected life.

With eyes closed and heart open to the symphony of nature, Soroush opened the Vial of Tranquility and released its contents into the air. The fragrance of the vial spread through the grove, carrying with it a sense of tranquillity and connection. As he stood in the midst of the fragrant mist, he felt a subtle shift—the rustling leaves and the whispers of the wind seemed to crescendo into a harmonious melody.

As dawn broke and painted the horizon with hues of pink and gold, Soroush's meditation gradually came to an end, leaving him standing in the amphitheatre bathed in a soft, ethereal light. He knew that the Grove of Whispers had granted him a gift—the realisation that nature was not just a collection of living things, but a symphony of voices and stories waiting to be heard.

With the Vial of Tranquility in his hand and a spirit illuminated by the essence of nature, Soroush returned to his village. He shared the tale of the "Grove of Whispers" and the revelations he had experienced with his fellow herbalists and seekers, reminding them that the connection between healer and earth was a dance of listening and understanding, and that the pursuit of harmony with nature was a symphony of respect and coexistence.

And so, dear listener, the story of Soroush and the "Grove of Whispers" teaches us that nature is a journey that transcends mere observation, that the bond between healer and earth is a dance of listening and understanding, and that the essence of interconnectedness is a timeless truth from the heart of ancient Persia.

The Starlight Nomad

Journeying Beyond the Horizon of Dreams

In a vast desert where dunes stretched like golden waves and the night sky shimmered with stars, lived a young nomad named Zara. Zara's eyes held the wonder of endless horizons, and her heart resonated with the mysteries of the cosmos.

One night, as Zara was gazing at the stars and tracing constellations with her fingers in the sand, an old astronomer with a staff adorned with celestial symbols approached her. The astronomer's eyes held the depth of the universe, and his presence seemed to carry the echoes of cosmic knowledge. He observed Zara's stargazing with a knowing smile and said, "Your eyes possess the skill to read the stars, but to truly understand the essence of the cosmos, you must journey to the Realm of Starlight."

Intrigued by the astronomer's words, Zara expressed her interest in undertaking the journey. The astronomer nodded and handed her a small telescope adorned with intricate engravings. "Carry this Telescope of Wanderings with you, and let it guide your path," he said. "Seek the Realm of Starlight, where the mysteries of the universe and the dreams of the wanderer intertwine."

With the Telescope of Wanderings in her hand and a heart brimming with curiosity, Zara set out on her journey to find the Realm of Starlight—a place whispered about in tales, said to be a sanctuary where stargazers were not just observers, but seekers of the cosmic truths woven into the fabric of existence. Guided by the constellations and the whispers of the desert winds, she journeyed through moonlit nights, crossed vast plains, and embraced the mysteries and revelations that her path held.

One evening, as the moon illuminated the desert with a silver glow and the stars above seemed to wink in approval, Zara arrived at the entrance of the Realm of Starlight. The air was crisp and tinged with the scent of night-blooming flowers. She noticed the realm's entrance, adorned with patterns that mirrored the constellations above.

As Zara stepped into the realm's central courtyard, she found herself surrounded by an ethereal luminescence—an aura that seemed to radiate from the very sky itself. She held up the Telescope of Wanderings, and as its engravings caught the moon's light, the realm's atmosphere shifted, becoming a haven where the mysteries of the cosmos seemed to come alive.

With a sense of awe, Zara moved deeper into the courtyard. She walked among sculptures that represented planets, passed through archways that depicted galaxies, and felt the presence of the universe enveloping her. As she moved among the cosmic symbols, she felt a connection—an interplay of energies that transcended the boundaries of time and space.

With the Telescope of Wanderings in her hand, Zara came upon an observatory—a domed structure with an opening that framed the vastness of the night sky. She climbed the steps and peered through the telescope, allowing her gaze to wander among the stars. As she adjusted the lens, distant galaxies came into view, stars revealed their secrets, and nebulae unfurled like cosmic tapestries.

With eyes focused on the celestial wonders, Zara felt a shift in the realm's energy—the patterns of the stars, the silent melodies of planets, and the whispers of galaxies all seemed to harmonise into a symphony of interconnected constellations.

As dawn broke and painted the horizon with hues of pink and gold, Zara's stargazing gradually came to an end, leaving her standing in the observatory bathed in a soft, ethereal light. She knew that the Realm of Starlight had granted her a gift—the realisation that the cosmos was not just a distant spectacle, but a living symphony of interconnected energies.

With the Telescope of Wanderings in her hand and a spirit illuminated by the essence of the cosmos, Zara returned to her desert home. She shared the tale of the "Realm of Starlight" and the revelations she had experienced with her fellow stargazers and seekers, reminding them that the connection between observer and universe was a dance of curiosity and understanding, and that the pursuit of cosmic wisdom was a symphony of exploration and interconnectedness.

And so, dear listener, the story of Zara and the "Realm of Starlight" teaches us that the cosmos is a journey that transcends mere observation, that the bond between stargazer and universe is a dance of curiosity and understanding, and that the essence of interconnectedness is a timeless truth from the heart of ancient Persia.

The Mirror of Compassion

Reflections that Heal the Heart

In a tranquil village surrounded by lush gardens and babbling brooks, lived a young healer named Laila. Laila's eyes held the depth of empathy, and her heart resonated with the sorrows and joys of those around her.

One day, as Laila was tending to a wounded bird in her garden, an old sage with a staff adorned with blossoms approached her. The sage's eyes held the serenity of still waters, and his presence seemed to carry the echoes of ancient wisdom. He observed Laila's caring actions with a knowing smile and said, "Your touch possesses the power to mend the broken, but to truly understand the essence of healing, you must journey to the Lake of Reflection."

Intrigued by the sage's words, Laila expressed her interest in undertaking the journey. The sage nodded and handed her a small mirror adorned with delicate engravings. "Carry this Mirror of Compassion with you, and let it guide your path," he said. "Seek the Lake of Reflection, where the depths of the heart and the ripples of kindness intertwine."

With the Mirror of Compassion in her hand and a heart brimming with compassion, Laila set out on her journey to find the Lake of Reflection—a place whispered about in stories, said to be a sanctuary where healers were not just mendors of bodies, but healers of souls through their empathy. Guided by the whispers of the wind and the gentle flow of the brooks, she journeyed through meadows, crossed bridges, and embraced the mysteries and revelations that her path held.

One evening, as the sun painted the sky with hues of gold and lavender, Laila arrived at the shores of the Lake of Reflection. The air was still, yet vibrant with the sounds of nature. She noticed the lake's shore, adorned with blossoms that seemed to bloom anew with every breeze.

As Laila gazed into the tranquil waters, she found herself surrounded by a soft radiance—a light that seemed to emanate from the very heart of the lake. She held up the Mirror of Compassion, and as its engravings caught the sunlight, the lake's surface began to shimmer and ripple, as if inviting her to peer into its depths.

With a heart full of empathy, Laila knelt by the lakeside and gazed into the water's depths. She saw images—moments of joy, instances of pain, and the faces of those she had healed. Each reflection held a story—a fragment of the human experience.

With the Mirror of Compassion in her hand, Laila touched the water's surface with her fingertips.
As her touch connected with the water, the images seemed to come alive, merging and converging into a symphony of emotions—a tapestry of memories and feelings woven by the people she had helped.

With closed eyes and heart open to the currents of humanity, Laila felt the lake's energy—the ripples, the whispers of lives intertwined, and the echoes of gratitude all seemed to harmonise into a chorus of interconnected hearts.

As dawn broke and painted the horizon with hues of pink and gold, Laila's meditation gradually came to an end, leaving her by the lake bathed in a soft, ethereal light. She knew that the Lake of Reflection had granted her a gift—the realisation that healing was not just a physical act, but a dance of empathy and understanding.

With the Mirror of Compassion in her hand and a spirit illuminated by the essence of healing, Laila returned to her village. She shared the tale of the "Lake of Reflection" and the revelations she had experienced with her fellow healers and caregivers, reminding them that the connection between healer and patient was a dance of empathy and understanding, and that the pursuit of healing was a symphony of compassion and interconnectedness.

And so, dear listener, the story of Laila and the "Lake of Reflection" teaches us that healing is a journey that transcends the mending of bodies, that the bond between healer and patient is a dance of empathy and understanding, and that the essence of compassion is a timeless truth from the heart of ancient Persia.

The Sands of Time

Lost and Found in the Hourglass of Eternity

In a desert oasis where palm trees swayed in the breeze and the shifting sands held the stories of centuries, lived a young historian named Farid. Farid's eyes held the curiosity of a seeker, and his heart resonated with the whispers of history.

One day, as Farid was poring over ancient scrolls in his study, an old sage with a staff adorned with symbols approached him. The sage's eyes held the depth of ages gone by, and his presence seemed to carry the echoes of forgotten chronicles. He observed Farid's research with a knowing smile and said, "Your pursuit of knowledge possesses the power to uncover truths, but to truly understand the essence of time, you must journey to the Chamber of Echoes."

Intrigued by the sage's words, Farid expressed his interest in undertaking the journey. The sage nodded and handed him an ornate hourglass adorned with intricate carvings. "Carry this Hourglass of Eternity with you, and let it guide your path," he said. "Seek the Chamber of Echoes, where the sands of history and the echoes of the past intertwine."

With the Hourglass of Eternity in his hand and a heart brimming with curiosity, Farid set out on his journey to find the Chamber of Echoes—a place whispered about in tales, said to be a sanctuary where historians were not just chroniclers, but travellers through time itself. Guided by the patterns of the stars and the winds that carried the secrets of the desert, he journeyed through shifting dunes, crossed ancient trails, and embraced the mysteries and revelations that his path held.

One evening, as the sun dipped below the horizon and the stars painted the sky with stories of their own, Farid arrived at the entrance of the Chamber of Echoes. The air was hushed, yet vibrant with the echoes of ages past. He noticed the chamber's entrance, adorned with symbols that seemed to shimmer like ancient calligraphy.

As Farid stepped into the chamber's heart, he found himself surrounded by an ethereal light—a radiance that seemed to come from the very walls themselves. He held up the Hourglass of Eternity, and as its carvings caught the ambient light, the chamber's atmosphere shifted, becoming a space where time's tapestry seemed to hang suspended.

With a sense of wonder, Farid moved deeper into the chamber. He walked among shelves of scrolls, passed by statues that depicted historical figures, and felt the resonance of centuries envelope him. As he moved among the relics, he felt a connection—an interplay of past and present that transcended the boundaries of eras.

With the Hourglass of Eternity in his hand, Farid came upon a mural—an intricate painting that depicted scenes from different epochs. He gazed at the mural and closed his eyes, allowing his thoughts to merge with the stories it held. He felt a shift in the chamber's energy—the stories, the whispers of forgotten voices, and the echoes of bygone eras all seemed to harmonise into a symphony of interconnected timelines.

With eyes closed and heart open to the currents of history, Farid turned the hourglass over. The sands within flowed in mesmerising patterns, like the river of time itself. As he watched, he felt a subtle shift—the sands of the hourglass and the echoes of the chamber seemed to blend, creating a harmony of timelines and experiences.

As dawn broke and painted the horizon with hues of gold and azure, Farid's meditation gradually came to an end, leaving him standing in the chamber bathed in a soft, ethereal light. He knew that the Chamber of Echoes had granted him a gift—the realisation that history was not just a collection of events, but a symphony of interconnected stories.

With the Hourglass of Eternity in his hand and a spirit illuminated by the essence of time, Farid returned to his oasis. He shared the tale of the "Chamber of Echoes" and the revelations he had experienced with his fellow historians and seekers, reminding them that the connection between historian and history was a dance of exploration and understanding, and that the pursuit of knowledge was a symphony of interconnected chronicles.

And so, dear listener, the story of Farid and the "Chamber of Echoes" teaches us that history is a journey that transcends the mere recording of events, that the bond between historian and history is a dance of exploration and understanding, and that the essence of time is a timeless truth from the heart of ancient Persia.

The Celestial Sculptor

Sculpting Destiny in the Stone of the Stars

In a city adorned with grand palaces and bustling markets, where the scent of exotic spices mingled with the rhythms of commerce and the laughter of children echoed through the streets, lived a young sculptor named Arash. Arash's eyes held the vision of an artist, and his heart resonated with the forms hidden within the stone.

One day, as Arash was shaping a block of marble into a figure that seemed to emerge from the very stone itself, an old artisan with a staff adorned with gemstones approached him. The artisan's eyes held the spark of creativity, and his presence seemed to carry the echoes of masterpieces long crafted. He observed Arash's work with a knowing smile and said, "Your hands possess the skill to shape matter, but to truly understand the essence of creation, you must journey to the Atelier of Stars."

Intrigued by the artisan's words, Arash expressed his interest in undertaking the journey. The artisan nodded and handed him a chisel adorned with intricate patterns. "Carry this Chisel of Visions with you, and let it guide your path," he said. "Seek the Atelier of Stars, where the visions of the mind and the artistry of the soul intertwine."

With the Chisel of Visions in his hand and a heart brimming with inspiration, Arash set out on his journey to find the Atelier of Stars—a place whispered about in legends, said to be a sanctuary where sculptors were not just craftsmen, but creators who harnessed the essence of the cosmos in their works. Guided by the constellations and the whispers of the night breeze, he journeyed through marketplaces, climbed hills, and embraced the mysteries and revelations that his path held.

One evening, as the sun cast its farewell glow upon the city and the stars began to appear like diamonds in the sky, Arash arrived at the entrance of the Atelier of Stars. The air was charged with creativity, like the hum of unseen muses. He noticed the atelier's entrance, adorned with shapes that seemed to dance in the twilight.

As Arash stepped into the atelier's interior, he found himself surrounded by an ethereal glow—a luminance that seemed to emanate from the very sculptures that adorned the space. He held up the Chisel of

Visions, and as its patterns caught the fading light, the atelier's atmosphere transformed, becoming a haven where artistic visions seemed to take on life.

With a sense of wonder, Arash moved deeper into the atelier. He walked among sculptures that seemed to capture the essence of the elements, passed by forms that depicted mythical beings, and felt the presence of creation envelop him.
As he moved among the sculptures, he felt a connection—an interplay of creativity and inspiration that transcended the boundaries of the tangible.

With the Chisel of Visions in his hand, Arash found himself before an open space—an empty pedestal that seemed to beckon to him. He gazed at the pedestal and closed his eyes, allowing his imagination to merge with the potential of the stone.
He felt a shift in the atelier's energy—the artistic visions, the whispers of artistic muses, and the echoes of untold tales all seemed to harmonise into a symphony of interconnected artistic endeavours.

With eyes closed and heart open to the wellspring of creativity, Arash lifted the Chisel of Visions and began to carve. The stone responded to his touch, yielding to his intentions as if guided by a cosmic force. As he chiselled, he felt a subtle shift—the stone and his chisel seemed to resonate, creating a harmony of artist and medium.

As dawn broke and painted the horizon with hues of orange and lavender, Arash's sculpting gradually came to an end, leaving him by the pedestal bathed in a soft, ethereal light. He knew that the Atelier of Stars had granted him a gift—the realisation that artistry was not just a craft, but a dance of visions brought to life.

With the Chisel of Visions in his hand and a spirit illuminated by the essence of creation, Arash returned to his city. He shared the tale of the "Atelier of Stars" and the revelations he had experienced with his fellow artists and dreamers, reminding them that the connection between sculptor and creation was a dance of visions and expression, and that the pursuit of artistic beauty was a symphony of imagination and interconnectedness.

And so, dear listener, the story of Arash and the "Atelier of Stars" teaches us that artistry is a journey that transcends mere craftsmanship, that the bond between creator and creation is a dance of visions and expression, and that the essence of cosmic artistry is a timeless truth from the heart of ancient Persia.

The Whispering Bazaar

Wonders Unveiled in the Labyrinth of Commerce

In a bustling bazaar where merchants displayed their wares and the air was alive with the symphony of haggling and laughter, lived a young trader named Leyla. Leyla's eyes held the insight of a negotiator, and her heart resonated with the melodies of the market.

One day, as Leyla was weaving through the stalls, an old merchant with a staff adorned with trinkets approached her. The merchant's eyes held the wisdom of countless deals, and his presence seemed to carry the echoes of trade routes traversed. He observed Leyla's transactions with a knowing smile and said, "Your skill in commerce possesses the power to shape destinies, but to truly understand the essence of exchange, you must journey to the Labyrinth of Whispers."

Intrigued by the merchant's words, Leyla expressed her interest in undertaking the journey. The merchant nodded and handed her a small coin adorned with intricate symbols. "Carry this Coin of Harmony with you, and let it guide your path," he said. "Seek the Labyrinth of Whispers, where the threads of fortune and the echoes of trade intertwine."

With the Coin of Harmony in her hand and a heart brimming with determination, Leyla set out on her journey to find the Labyrinth of Whispers—a place spoken of in tales, said to be a labyrinthine marketplace where traders were not just negotiators, but dancers in the grand tapestry of commerce. Guided by the myriad sounds of the bazaar and the patterns of transactions, she journeyed through alleyways, crossed thresholds, and embraced the mysteries and revelations that her path held.

One evening, as the sun cast long shadows upon the bazaar and the lanterns began to glow like stars on the ground, Leyla arrived at the entrance of the Labyrinth of Whispers. The air was a blend of fragrances and voices, forming an enchanting symphony. She noticed the labyrinth's entrance, adorned with patterns that seemed to shift with the movement of the lantern light.

As Leyla stepped into the labyrinth's bustling heart, she found herself surrounded by a kaleidoscope of colours—a panorama that seemed to arise from the vibrant wares displayed by countless vendors.

She held up the Coin of Harmony, and as its symbols caught the lantern light, the labyrinth's atmosphere transformed, becoming a space where commerce and culture seemed to intermingle.

With a sense of anticipation, Leyla moved deeper into the labyrinth. She wove through stalls of spices, brushed against fabrics that told stories of distant lands, and felt the rhythm of the marketplace envelop her. As she moved among the vendors, she felt a connection—an interplay of transactions and experiences that transcended the boundaries of individual deals.

With the Coin of Harmony in her hand, Leyla came upon a central plaza—a bustling square where the very essence of the Labyrinth of Whispers seemed to converge.
She gazed at the plaza and closed her eyes, allowing her senses to merge with the symphony of the bazaar. She felt a shift in the labyrinth's energy—the sounds of haggling, the laughter of traders, and the echoes of deals struck all seemed to harmonise into a chorus of interconnected fortunes.

With eyes closed and heart open to the rhythms of exchange, Leyla tossed the Coin of Harmony into a central fountain. As the coin descended into the water, she felt a resonance—the coin's journey and the marketplace's symphony seemed to align, creating a harmony of transactions and connections.

As dawn broke and painted the horizon with hues of gold and azure, Leyla's contemplation gradually came to an end, leaving her in the plaza bathed in a soft, ethereal light. She knew that the Labyrinth of Whispers had granted her a gift—the realisation that commerce was not just about transactions, but a dance of interconnected fortunes.

With the Coin of Harmony in her hand and a spirit illuminated by the essence of exchange, Leyla returned to her bazaar. She shared the tale of the "Labyrinth of Whispers" and the revelations she had experienced with her fellow traders and barterers, reminding them that the connection between buyer and seller was a dance of transactions and understandings, and that the pursuit of prosperous commerce was a symphony of harmony and interconnectedness.

And so, dear listener, the story of Leyla and the "Labyrinth of Whispers" teaches us that commerce is a journey that transcends the exchange of goods, that the bond between trader and market is a dance of transactions and understandings, and that the essence of harmonious exchange is a timeless truth from the heart of ancient Persia.

The Serpent's Wisdom

Enlightenment Found in the Eyes of the Reptile

In a tranquil village nestled among emerald hills and serene ponds, lived a young scholar named Darius. Darius's eyes held the inquisitiveness of a seeker, and his heart resonated with the enigmas of life.

One day, as Darius was delving into ancient texts beneath a shaded tree, an old sage with a staff adorned with feathers approached him. The sage's eyes held the serenity of still waters, and his presence seemed to carry the echoes of ancient truths. He observed Darius's studies with a knowing smile and said, "Your pursuit of knowledge possesses the power to unveil mysteries, but to truly understand the essence of wisdom, you must journey to the Grove of Whispers."

Intrigued by the sage's words, Darius expressed his interest in undertaking the journey. The sage nodded and handed him a small serpent-shaped pendant. "Carry this Serpent of Enlightenment with you, and let it guide your path," he said. "Seek the Grove of Whispers, where the secrets of life and the whispers of the earth intertwine."

With the Serpent of Enlightenment in his hand and a heart brimming with curiosity, Darius set out on his journey to find the Grove of Whispers—a place spoken of in legends, said to be a sanctuary where seekers were not just scholars, but listeners to the voices of nature itself. Guided by the rustling leaves and the murmurs of the wind, he journeyed through meadows, crossed streams, and embraced the mysteries and revelations that his path held.

One evening, as the sun dipped below the horizon and the stars emerged like lanterns in the sky, Darius arrived at the entrance of the Grove of Whispers. The air was alive with the sounds of crickets and the soft rustling of leaves. He noticed the grove's entrance, adorned with symbols that seemed to shimmer like ancient glyphs.

As Darius stepped into the grove's heart, he found himself surrounded by a tranquil aura—a presence that seemed to come from the very earth itself. He held up the Serpent of Enlightenment, and as its pendant caught the moon's glow, the grove's atmosphere shifted, becoming a haven where the wisdom of nature seemed to awaken.

With a sense of reverence, Darius moved deeper into the grove. He walked among trees that stood like guardians of ancient secrets, touched the petals of flowers that whispered their tales, and felt the heartbeat of the earth beneath his feet. As he moved among the flora, he felt a connection—an interplay of energies that transcended the boundaries of human understanding.
With the Serpent of Enlightenment in his hand, Darius came upon a natural altar—a circular clearing where the very essence of the Grove of Whispers seemed to converge. He gazed at the altar and closed his eyes, allowing his thoughts to merge with the tranquillity of the grove. He felt a shift in the grove's energy—the rustling leaves, the soft murmur of the brook, and the echoes of the creatures all seemed to harmonise into a symphony of interconnected existence.

With eyes closed and heart open to the symphony of nature, Darius held the Serpent of Enlightenment to his heart. As he did, he felt a sense of unity—a resonance with the world around him. In that moment of profound connection, he experienced a shift—the serpent pendant seemed to glow, and the grove's energy embraced him like a warm embrace.

As dawn broke and painted the horizon with hues of pink and gold, Darius's meditation gradually came to an end, leaving him in the grove's heart bathed in a soft, ethereal light. He knew that the Grove of Whispers had granted him a gift—the realisation that wisdom was not just found in books, but in the harmonious symphony of the earth itself.

With the Serpent of Enlightenment in his hand and a spirit illuminated by the essence of wisdom, Darius returned to his village. He shared the tale of the "Grove of Whispers" and the revelations he had experienced with his fellow scholars and truth-seekers, reminding them that the connection between seeker and nature was a dance of listening and understanding, and that the pursuit of wisdom was a symphony of interconnected revelations.

And so, dear listener, the story of Darius and the "Grove of Whispers" teaches us that wisdom is a journey that transcends the pages of books, that the bond between seeker and nature is a dance of listening and understanding, and that the essence of enlightenment is a timeless truth from the heart of ancient Persia.

The Phoenix's Flight

Rebirth Found in the Embrace of the Flames

In a city adorned with towering minarets and bustling markets, where the songs of merchants mingled with the fragrance of spices and the laughter of children echoed through the streets, lived a young artisan named Layla. Layla's eyes held the creativity of a maker, and her heart resonated with the magic of transformation.

One day, as Layla was shaping molten metal into intricate patterns in her workshop, an old alchemist with a staff adorned with alchemical symbols approached her. The alchemist's eyes held the shimmer of ancient secrets, and his presence seemed to carry the echoes of hidden formulas. He observed Layla's craft with a knowing smile and said, "Your hands possess the skill to mould materials, but to truly understand the essence of transformation, you must journey to the Forge of Renewal."

Intrigued by the alchemist's words, Layla expressed her interest in undertaking the journey. The alchemist nodded and handed her a small vial filled with liquid gold. "Carry this Elixir of Rebirth with you, and let it guide your path," he said. "Seek the Forge of Renewal, where the flames of change and the echoes of creation intertwine."

With the Elixir of Rebirth in her hand and a heart brimming with wonder, Layla set out on her journey to find the Forge of Renewal—a place spoken of in myths, said to be a sanctuary where artisans were not just crafters, but weavers of the cosmic tapestry of renewal. Guided by the flicker of stars and the wind's whispers, she journeyed through alleys, passed by ancient ruins, and embraced the mysteries and revelations that her path held.

One evening, as the sun painted the sky with shades of crimson and gold, Layla arrived at the entrance of the Forge of Renewal. The air was alive with the dance of flames and the murmurs of the wind. She noticed the forge's entrance, adorned with patterns that seemed to shimmer like molten metal.

As Layla stepped into the forge's heart, she found herself surrounded by a warm glow—an ambiance that seemed to emanate from the very flames that danced in the air. She held up the Elixir of Rebirth, and as the liquid gold caught the firelight, the forge's atmosphere shifted, becoming a space where the alchemy of creation seemed to come to life.

With a sense of reverence, Layla moved deeper into the forge. She observed tools that lay ready for artisans to shape their visions, felt the heat of the fires that fueled their craft, and sensed the heartbeat of transformation that resonated within the walls. As she moved among the artefacts, she felt a connection—an interplay of energies that transcended the boundaries of the mundane.

With the Elixir of Rebirth in her hand, Layla found herself before an anvil—an ancient block of stone that bore the marks of countless creations. She gazed at the anvil and closed her eyes, allowing her thoughts to merge with the potential of her craft. She felt a shift in the forge's energy—the flames, the echoes of creations past, and the aspirations of artisans all seemed to harmonise into a symphony of interconnected artistry.

With eyes closed and heart open to the symphony of transformation, Layla dipped her fingers into the Elixir of Rebirth and touched the anvil's surface. As she did, a wave of warmth washed over her, and the alchemical elixir seemed to meld with the essence of the forge itself. In that moment of profound connection, she experienced a shift—the flames danced higher, and the forge's energy embraced her like an old friend.

As dawn broke and painted the horizon with hues of orange and lavender, Layla's contemplation gradually came to an end, leaving her by the anvil bathed in a soft, ethereal light. She knew that the Forge of Renewal had granted her a gift—the realisation that transformation was not just a process, but a dance of creation's rhythms.

With the Elixir of Rebirth in her hand and a spirit illuminated by the essence of change, Layla returned to her city. She shared the tale of the "Forge of Renewal" and the revelations she had experienced with her fellow artisans and creators, reminding them that the connection between maker and creation was a dance of inspiration and shaping, and that the pursuit of artistic transformation was a symphony of renewal and interconnectedness.

And so, dear listener, the story of Layla and the "Forge of Renewal" teaches us that transformation is a journey that transcends the shaping of materials, that the bond between artisan and creation is a dance of inspiration and renewal, and that the essence of alchemical change is a timeless truth from the heart of ancient Persia.

The Starlit Lovers

Cosmic Romance in the Tapestry of the Night

In a desert oasis where the night sky sparkled with constellations and the fragrance of blooming flowers mingled with the soft breeze, lived a young astronomer named Amir. Amir's eyes held the wonder of a dreamer, and his heart resonated with the mysteries of the universe.

One evening, as Amir was gazing through his telescope, an old stargazer with a staff adorned with celestial symbols approached him. The stargazer's eyes held the wisdom of starlight, and his presence seemed to carry the echoes of forgotten cosmic tales. He observed Amir's observation with a knowing smile and said, "Your pursuit of the stars possesses the power to unlock celestial stories, but to truly understand the essence of cosmic connection, you must journey to the Nexus of Stars."

Intrigued by the stargazer's words, Amir expressed his interest in undertaking the journey. The stargazer nodded and handed him a small crystal amulet reflecting the night sky. "Carry this Amulet of Unity with you, and let it guide your path," he said. "Seek the Nexus of Stars, where the threads of fate and the echoes of love intertwine."

With the Amulet of Unity in his hand and a heart brimming with anticipation, Amir set out on his journey to find the Nexus of Stars—a place spoken of in lore, said to be a sanctuary where astronomers were not just observers, but seekers of cosmic connections. Guided by the shimmering constellations and the whispered secrets of the night, he journeyed through moonlit dunes, crossed shimmering rivers, and embraced the mysteries and revelations that his path held.

One night, as the moon bathed the desert in silver and the stars were woven into a tapestry of shimmering light, Amir arrived at the entrance of the Nexus of Stars. The air was still, yet alive with the energies of the cosmos. He noticed the nexus's entrance, adorned with patterns that seemed to glimmer like galaxies colliding.

As Amir stepped into the nexus's heart, he found himself surrounded by a luminous aura—an emanation that seemed to come from the very starlight that danced in the heavens above. He held up the Amulet of Unity, and as its crystal facets caught the starlight, the nexus's ambiance shifted, becoming a realm where the celestial and the earthly seemed to merge.

With a sense of reverence, Amir moved deeper into the nexus. He walked among pathways that seemed to trace the movements of the planets, reached out to touch formations that resembled galaxies, and felt the presence of the cosmos embrace him. As he moved among the cosmic formations, he felt a connection—an interplay of energies that transcended the boundaries of time and space.

With the Amulet of Unity in his hand, Amir reached a central clearing—a place where the very essence of the Nexus of Stars seemed to converge. He gazed at the clearing and closed his eyes, allowing his thoughts to merge with the astral melodies of the universe.
He felt a shift in the nexus's energy—the twinkling stars, the echoes of celestial events, and the whispers of cosmic love all seemed to harmonise into a symphony of interconnected destinies.

With eyes closed and heart open to the cosmic harmony, Amir clasped the Amulet of Unity to his chest. As he did, he felt a resonance—the amulet's facets seemed to glow, and the nexus's energy enveloped him like a cosmic embrace.

As dawn broke and painted the horizon with hues of pink and gold, Amir's meditation gradually came to an end, leaving him in the nexus's heart bathed in a soft, ethereal light. He knew that the Nexus of Stars had granted him a gift—the realisation that the connection between the heavens and the earth was not just astronomical, but a dance of celestial unity.

With the Amulet of Unity in his hand and a spirit illuminated by the essence of cosmic connection, Amir returned to his oasis. He shared the tale of the "Nexus of Stars" and the revelations he had experienced with his fellow astronomers and star gazers, reminding them that the bond between stargazer and the universe was a dance of cosmic unity, and that the pursuit of celestial insight was a symphony of interconnected destinies.

And so, dear listener, the story of Amir and the "Nexus of Stars" teaches us that the cosmos is a journey that transcends mere observation, that the bond between stargazer and the universe is a dance of cosmic unity, and that the essence of celestial connection is a timeless truth from the heart of ancient Persia.

The Weaver's Threads

Tapestries of Life Woven in the Loom of Destiny

In a serene village nestled among rolling hills and orchards, lived a young weaver named Parisa. Parisa's eyes held the vision of an artist, and her heart resonated with the rhythms of creation.

One day, as Parisa was weaving intricate patterns into a tapestry, an old storyteller with a staff adorned with feathers approached her. The storyteller's eyes held the depths of a thousand tales, and his presence seemed to carry the echoes of forgotten chronicles. He observed Parisa's work with a knowing smile and said, "Your hands possess the skill to intertwine threads, but to truly understand the essence of creation, you must journey to the Loom of Destiny."

Intrigued by the storyteller's words, Parisa expressed her interest in undertaking the journey. The storyteller nodded and handed her a spool of radiant silk thread. "Carry this Thread of Unity with you, and let it guide your path," he said. "Seek the Loom of Destiny, where the threads of life and the echoes of fate intertwine."

With the Thread of Unity in her hand and a heart brimming with curiosity, Parisa set out on her journey to find the Loom of Destiny—a place whispered about in fables, said to be a sanctum where weavers were not just crafters, but architects of the grand tapestry of existence. Guided by the rustling leaves and the harmonies of the wind, she journeyed through meadows, passed by ancient ruins, and embraced the mysteries and revelations that her path held.

One evening, as the sun cast its golden hues upon the landscape and the stars began to emerge like gems in the sky, Parisa arrived at the entrance of the Loom of Destiny. The air was a gentle symphony of rustling leaves and distant melodies. She noticed the loom's entrance, adorned with patterns that seemed to shimmer like the threads she wove.

As Parisa stepped into the loom's heart, she found herself surrounded by a serene aura—a presence that seemed to come from the very patterns woven into the fabric of existence. She held up the Thread of Unity, and as its radiance caught the last rays of sunlight, the loom's ambiance shifted, becoming a haven where creation and destiny seemed to blend.

With a sense of reverence, Parisa moved deeper into the loom. She observed the loom's intricate mechanisms, touched threads that held the colours of seasons, and felt the pulse of existence beneath her fingertips. As she moved among the patterns, she felt a connection—an interplay of energies that transcended the boundaries of individual lives.

With the Thread of Unity in her hand, Parisa came upon a central platform—an open space where the very essence of the Loom of Destiny seemed to converge. She gazed at the platform and closed her eyes, allowing her thoughts to merge with the symphony of life's harmonies. She felt a shift in the loom's energy—the whispers of stories, the echoes of generations, and the connections of lives all seemed to harmonise into a chorus of interconnected existence.

With eyes closed and heart open to the symphony of creation, Parisa stepped onto the platform. As she did, a wave of energy swept over her, and the radiant silk thread seemed to resonate with the essence of the loom itself. In that moment of profound connection, she experienced a shift—the threads seemed to glow, and the loom's energy embraced her like an ancient embrace.

As dawn broke and painted the horizon with hues of pink and gold, Parisa's meditation gradually came to an end, leaving her on the platform bathed in a soft, ethereal light. She knew that the Loom of Destiny had granted her a gift—the realisation that creation was not just a craft, but a dance of interconnected lives.

With the Thread of Unity in her hand and a spirit illuminated by the essence of existence, Parisa returned to her village. She shared the tale of the "Loom of Destiny" and the revelations she had experienced with her fellow weavers and creators, reminding them that the bond between craftsman and creation was a dance of interconnected lives, and that the pursuit of artistic harmony was a symphony of woven destinies.

And so, dear listener, the story of Parisa and the "Loom of Destiny" teaches us that creation is a journey that transcends mere craftsmanship, that the bond between weaver and creation is a dance of interconnected lives, and that the essence of existence's tapestry is a timeless truth from the heart of ancient Persia.

The Oracle's Veil

Prophecy Unveiled in the Sanctuary of Secrets

In a city adorned with opulent palaces and gardens, where the melodies of musicians blended with the aromas of exotic spices, lived a young seeker named Farid. Farid's eyes held the yearning of a truth-seeker, and his heart resonated with the mysteries of the unseen.

One day, as Farid was exploring ancient manuscripts in a hidden library, an old sage with a staff adorned with enigmatic symbols approached him. The sage's eyes held the depth of ancient knowledge, and his presence seemed to carry the echoes of unspoken prophecies. He observed Farid's studies with a knowing smile and said, "Your pursuit of hidden truths possesses the power to unveil prophecies, but to truly understand the essence of foresight, you must journey to the Sanctuary of Visions."

Intrigued by the sage's words, Farid expressed his interest in undertaking the journey. The sage nodded and handed him a small crystal sphere filled with swirling mist. "Carry this Sphere of Insight with you, and let it guide your path," he said. "Seek the Sanctuary of Visions, where the currents of time and the echoes of destiny intertwine."

With the Sphere of Insight in his hand and a heart brimming with anticipation, Farid set out on his journey to find the Sanctuary of Visions—a place whispered about in tales, said to be a haven where seekers were not just scholars, but listeners to the prophecies of the ages. Guided by the wind's whispers and the echoes of forgotten echoes, he journeyed through ancient streets, passed through arched gateways, and embraced the mysteries and revelations that his path held.

One evening, as the sun cast its golden glow upon the city and the lanterns began to flicker like stars on the ground, Farid arrived at the entrance of the Sanctuary of Visions. The air was hushed, yet alive with the currents of anticipation. He noticed the sanctuary's entrance, adorned with patterns that seemed to shimmer like ripples on water.

As Farid stepped into the sanctuary's interior, he found himself surrounded by an ethereal aura—an ambiance that seemed to emanate from the very currents of time that flowed within the walls. He held up the Sphere of Insight, and as its mist caught the warm light, the sanctuary's atmosphere shifted, becoming a realm where past, present, and future seemed to intertwine.

With a sense of reverence, Farid moved deeper into the sanctuary. He walked among alcoves that held relics of forgotten ages, brushed his fingers against inscriptions that bore tales of the yet-to-come, and felt the weight of destiny upon his shoulders. As he moved among the artefacts, he felt a connection—an interplay of energies that transcended the boundaries of ordinary perception.

With the Sphere of Insight in his hand, Farid approached a central dais—a circular platform where the very essence of the Sanctuary of Visions seemed to converge. He gazed at the dais and closed his eyes, allowing his thoughts to merge with the currents of time's whispers. He felt a shift in the sanctuary's energy—the echoes of ages past, the pulse of the present moment, and the mysteries of futures unseen all seemed to harmonise into a symphony of interconnected destinies.

With eyes closed and heart open to the symphony of prophecies, Farid held the Sphere of Insight before him. As he did, he felt a resonance—the mist within the sphere seemed to swirl and dance, and the sanctuary's energy enveloped him like a gentle embrace.

As dawn broke and painted the horizon with hues of pink and gold, Farid's meditation gradually came to an end, leaving him on the dais bathed in a soft, ethereal light. He knew that the Sanctuary of Visions had granted him a gift—the realisation that prophecy was not just a divination, but a dance of interconnected destinies.

With the Sphere of Insight in his hand and a spirit illuminated by the essence of foresight, Farid returned to his city. He shared the tale of the "Sanctuary of Visions" and the revelations he had experienced with his fellow seekers and truth-seekers, reminding them that the bond between seeker and prophecy was a dance of interconnected destinies, and that the pursuit of truth's unveiling was a symphony of insight and revelation.

And so, dear listener, the story of Farid and the "Sanctuary of Visions" teaches us that foresight is a journey that transcends mere divination, that the bond between seeker and prophecy is a dance of interconnected destinies, and that the essence of truth's unveiling is a timeless truth from the heart of ancient Persia.

The Oasis Oracle

Reflections of Destiny Found in the Waters of Fate

In a desert oasis where the palm trees swayed in the breeze and the tranquil waters mirrored the expanse of the sky, lived a young oracle named Soraya. Soraya's eyes held the depth of a seer, and her heart resonated with the currents of fate.

One day, as Soraya was gazing into the still waters, an old sage with a staff adorned with symbols approached her. The sage's eyes held the knowing of ages, and his presence seemed to carry the echoes of countless destinies. He observed Soraya's reflection-gazing with a knowing smile and said, "Your pursuit of the waters' mysteries possesses the power to unveil reflections of fate, but to truly understand the essence of destiny, you must journey to the Pool of Reflections."

Intrigued by the sage's words, Soraya expressed her interest in undertaking the journey. The sage nodded and handed her a small vial containing shimmering liquid. "Carry this Elixir of Reflection with you, and let it guide your path," he said. "Seek the Pool of Reflections, where the ripples of time and the echoes of destinies intertwine."

With the Elixir of Reflection in her hand and a heart brimming with anticipation, Soraya set out on her journey to find the Pool of Reflections—a place spoken of in whispers, said to be a haven where oracles were not just diviners, but listeners to the whispers of fate's reflection. Guided by the wind's caress and the songs of desert birds, she journeyed through sand dunes, crossed the river's embrace, and embraced the mysteries and revelations that her path held.

One evening, as the sun dipped below the horizon and the stars began to adorn the darkening sky, Soraya arrived at the entrance of the Pool of Reflections. The air was still, yet alive with the gentle sighs of the waters. She noticed the pool's entrance, adorned with patterns that seemed to shimmer like the ripples she sought.

As Soraya stepped to the edge of the pool, she found herself surrounded by a tranquil aura—an ambiance that seemed to come from the very waters that mirrored the heavens. She held up the Elixir of Reflection, and as the liquid caught the fading light, the pool's surface shifted, becoming a realm where the reflections of the world and the echoes of destinies seemed to intertwine.

With a sense of reverence, Soraya kneeled by the pool's edge. She observed the reflections that danced upon the waters, felt the depth of the ripples that held the stories of lives, and sensed the currents of fate beneath her fingertips. As she gazed into the pool, she felt a connection—an interplay of energies that transcended the boundaries of mortal vision.

With the Elixir of Reflection in her hand, Soraya dipped her fingers into the vial and let a drop fall onto the pool's surface. As the elixir merged with the waters, a gentle ripple spread across the pool. In that moment of profound connection, she experienced a shift—the ripples seemed to glow, and the pool's energy embraced her like a timeless current.

As dawn broke and painted the horizon with hues of pink and gold, Soraya's reflection-gazing gradually came to an end, leaving her by the pool bathed in a soft, ethereal light. She knew that the Pool of Reflections had granted her a gift—the realisation that destiny was not just a path, but a dance of interconnected lives.

With the Elixir of Reflection in her hand and a spirit illuminated by the essence of fate, Soraya returned to her oasis. She shared the tale of the "Pool of Reflections" and the revelations she had experienced with her fellow seers and visionaries, reminding them that the bond between oracle and fate was a dance of interconnected reflections, and that the pursuit of destiny's whispers was a symphony of insight and connection.

And so, dear listener, the story of Soraya and the "Pool of Reflections" teaches us that destiny is a journey that transcends mere foresight, that the bond between seer and fate is a dance of interconnected reflections, and that the essence of destiny's embrace is a timeless truth from the heart of ancient Persia.

The Enchanted Lute

Melodies of Magic Woven in the Strings of Fate

In a city of winding alleys and mosaic-adorned walls, where the melodies of musicians flowed like rivers and the fragrances of exotic teas wafted through the air, lived a young minstrel named Ramin. Ramin's eyes held the fire of a storyteller, and his heart resonated with the harmonies of enchantment.

One day, as Ramin was strumming his lute beneath an arched arcade, an old sage with a staff adorned with mystical symbols approached him. The sage's eyes held the luminance of ancient spells, and his presence seemed to carry the echoes of otherworldly verses. He observed Ramin's performance with a knowing smile and said, "Your melodies possess the power to awaken enchantments, but to truly understand the essence of magic, you must journey to the Grove of Melodies."

Intrigued by the sage's words, Ramin expressed his interest in undertaking the journey. The sage nodded and handed him a small crystal plectrum that shimmered like starlight. "Carry this Plectrum of Harmony with you, and let it guide your path," he said. "Seek the Grove of Melodies, where the harmonies of the world and the echoes of enchantments intertwine."

With the Plectrum of Harmony in his hand and a heart brimming with wonder, Ramin set out on his journey to find the Grove of Melodies—a place spoken of in legends, said to be a haven where minstrels were not just musicians, but weavers of the magical harmonies of existence. Guided by the rustling leaves and the whispers of ancient verses, he journeyed through bustling markets, passed by mystical ruins, and embraced the mysteries and revelations that his path held.

One night, as the moon bathed the world in silver and the stars shimmered like jewels in the sky, Ramin arrived at the entrance of the Grove of Melodies. The air was alive with the echoes of distant songs and the rustling of leaves. He noticed the grove's entrance, adorned with patterns that seemed to shimmer like intricate musical notations.

As Ramin stepped into the grove's heart, he found himself surrounded by a serene aura—an ambiance that seemed to come from the very melodies that danced in the breeze. He held up the Plectrum of Harmony, and as its crystal facets caught the moonlight, the grove's atmosphere shifted, becoming a sanctuary where the harmonies of existence and the echoes of enchantments seemed to intertwine.

With a sense of reverence, Ramin moved deeper into the grove. He observed the natural formations that seemed to resonate with musical rhythms, reached out to touch the trees that whispered melodies of ages past, and felt the magic of music flow through the air. As he moved among the arboreal wonders, he felt a connection—an interplay of energies that transcended the boundaries of the mundane.

With the Plectrum of Harmony in his hand, Ramin found himself before a natural stage—a clearing amidst the trees where the very essence of the Grove of Melodies seemed to converge.
He gazed at the stage and closed his eyes, allowing his thoughts to merge with the harmonies of existence. He felt a shift in the grove's energy—the echoes of ancient songs, the vibrations of the world's heartbeat, and the symphonies of enchantment all seemed to harmonise into a melody of interconnected magic.

With eyes closed and heart open to the symphony of magic, Ramin raised the Plectrum of Harmony to his lute's strings. As he strummed, the crystal plectrum resonated with the melodies of the grove, and the very air seemed to shimmer with ethereal light. In that moment of profound connection, he experienced a shift—the melodies seemed to meld, and the grove's energy embraced him like an enchanting embrace.

As dawn broke and painted the horizon with hues of gold and orange, Ramin's performance gradually came to an end, leaving him on the stage bathed in a soft, ethereal light. He knew that the Grove of Melodies had granted him a gift—the realisation that magic was not just a spell, but a dance of interconnected harmonies.

With the Plectrum of Harmony in his hand and a spirit illuminated by the essence of enchantment, Ramin returned to his city. He shared the tale of the "Grove of Melodies" and the revelations he had experienced with his fellow minstrels and musicians, reminding them that the bond between musician and melody was a dance of interconnected harmonies, and that the pursuit of enchantment's symphony was a chorus of magic and unity.

And so, dear listener, the story of Ramin and the "Grove of Melodies" teaches us that enchantment is a journey that transcends mere performance, that the bond between minstrel and melody is a dance of interconnected harmonies, and that the essence of magical music is a timeless truth from the heart of ancient Persia.

The Whispering Sands

Secrets of the Desert Unveiled in the Echoes of Time

In a land where endless dunes stretched like waves frozen in time, lived a young nomad named Zara. Zara's eyes held the curiosity of an explorer, and her heart resonated with the mysteries of the desert.

One day, as Zara was traversing the shifting sands, an old sage with a staff adorned with desert gems approached her.

The sage's eyes held the wisdom of ages, and his presence seemed to carry the echoes of forgotten tales. He observed Zara's footsteps with a knowing smile and said, "Your journey across these sands possesses the power to unveil ancient secrets, but to truly understand the essence of the desert, you must journey to the Echoing Oasis."

Intrigued by the sage's words, Zara expressed her interest in undertaking the journey. The sage nodded and handed her a small vial filled with luminous sand. "Carry this Sands of Echo with you, and let it guide your path," he said. "Seek the Echoing Oasis, where the whispers of time and the echoes of stories intertwine."

With the Sands of Echo in her hand and a heart brimming with anticipation, Zara set out on her journey to find the Echoing Oasis—a place spoken of in whispers, said to be a sanctuary where nomads were not just travellers, but listeners to the desert's secrets. Guided by the wind's caress and the songs of desert creatures, she journeyed through golden dunes, crossed meandering paths, and embraced the mysteries and revelations that her path held.

One night, as the moonlit dunes shimmered like silver oceans and the stars blinked like distant lanterns, Zara arrived at the entrance of the Echoing Oasis. The air was calm, yet alive with the soft rustling of palm fronds. She noticed the oasis's entrance, adorned with patterns that seemed to shimmer like mirages in the distance.

As Zara stepped into the oasis's heart, she found herself surrounded by a tranquil aura—an ambiance that seemed to come from the very whispers carried by the desert winds. She held up the Sands of Echo, and as the luminous sand caught the moonlight, the oasis's atmosphere shifted, becoming a haven where time's echoes and the stories of ages seemed to intertwine.

With a sense of reverence, Zara moved deeper into the oasis. She walked among the palm trees that swayed like dancers, touched the cool waters that held reflections of forgotten tales, and felt the presence of stories carried by the desert's breath. As she moved among the oasis's wonders, she felt a connection—an interplay of energies that transcended the boundaries of everyday existence.

With the Sands of Echo in her hand, Zara reached a central clearing—a space where the very essence of the Echoing Oasis seemed to converge. She gazed at the clearing and closed her eyes, allowing her thoughts to merge with the desert's ancient songs.
She felt a shift in the oasis's energy—the echoes of forgotten tales, the whispers of travellers, and the reverberations of time all seemed to harmonise into a symphony of interconnected stories.

With eyes closed and heart open to the symphony of desert echoes, Zara released a handful of the Sands of Echo into the wind. As the luminous grains dispersed, a soft, melodious echo spread through the oasis. In that moment of profound connection, she experienced a shift—the echoes seemed to linger, and the oasis's energy embraced her like a timeless embrace.

As dawn broke and painted the horizon with hues of orange and gold, Zara's contemplation gradually came to an end, leaving her in the oasis's heart bathed in a soft, ethereal light. She knew that the Echoing Oasis had granted her a gift—the realisation that the desert was not just a landscape, but a dance of interconnected stories.

With the Sands of Echo in her hand and a spirit illuminated by the essence of desert secrets, Zara returned to her nomadic camp. She shared the tale of the "Echoing Oasis" and the revelations she had experienced with her fellow travellers and explorers, reminding them that the bond between nomad and desert was a dance of interconnected stories, and that the pursuit of the desert's whispers was a symphony of wisdom and unity.

And so, dear listener, the story of Zara and the "Echoing Oasis" teaches us that the desert is a journey that transcends mere landscapes, that the bond between nomad and desert is a dance of interconnected stories, and that the essence of desert wisdom is a timeless truth from the heart of ancient Persia.

The Moonlit Ciphers

Unravelling Secrets in the Embrace of Lunar Mysteries

In a city where moonlight bathed the cobblestone streets and the fragrance of spices filled the air, lived a young scholar named Darius. Darius's eyes held the sparkle of an investigator, and his heart resonated with the enigmas of the night.

One evening, as Darius was poring over ancient manuscripts in a candlelit library, an old sage with a staff adorned with celestial symbols approached him. The sage's eyes held the luminescence of stars, and his presence seemed to carry the echoes of forgotten riddles. He observed Darius's studies with a knowing smile and said, "Your pursuit of hidden knowledge possesses the power to unveil mysteries, but to truly understand the essence of wisdom, you must journey to the Celestial Observatory."

Intrigued by the sage's words, Darius expressed his interest in undertaking the journey. The sage nodded and handed him a small parchment adorned with cryptic marks. "Carry this Cipher of Lunar Secrets with you, and let it guide your path," he said. "Seek the Celestial Observatory, where the dance of the stars and the echoes of enigmas intertwine."

With the Cipher of Lunar Secrets in his hand and a heart brimming with curiosity, Darius set out on his journey to find the Celestial Observatory—a place spoken of in whispers, said to be a sanctum where scholars were not just learners, but unravelers of the universe's mysteries. Guided by the moon's silver radiance and the whispers of the night, he journeyed through moonlit avenues, passed by ancient towers, and embraced the mysteries and revelations that his path held.

One night, as the moon cast its silvery glow upon the city and the constellations adorned the night sky like jewels on velvet, Darius arrived at the entrance of the Celestial Observatory. The air was hushed, yet alive with the quiet hum of cosmic energies. He noticed the observatory's entrance, adorned with patterns that seemed to shimmer like stardust.

As Darius stepped into the observatory's interior, he found himself surrounded by an ethereal aura—an ambiance that seemed to come from the very stars that adorned the sky. He held up the Cipher of Lunar Secrets, and as the cryptic marks caught the moon's glow, the observatory's atmosphere shifted, becoming a haven where cosmic movements and the mysteries of the ages seemed to intertwine.

With a sense of reverence, Darius moved deeper into the observatory. He observed the celestial instruments that measured the dance of planets, reached out to touch the telescopes that gazed into the depths of space, and felt the presence of cosmic enigmas in the air. As he moved among the observatory's wonders, he felt a connection—an interplay of energies that transcended the boundaries of earthly knowledge.

With the Cipher of Lunar Secrets in his hand, Darius approached a central dome—a chamber where the very essence of the Celestial Observatory seemed to converge. He gazed at the dome and closed his eyes, allowing his thoughts to merge with the whispers of the night sky. He felt a shift in the observatory's energy—the movements of celestial bodies, the patterns of constellations, and the riddles of the cosmos all seemed to harmonise into a symphony of interconnected wisdom.

With eyes closed and heart open to the symphony of cosmic mysteries, Darius held the Cipher of Lunar Secrets before him. As he did, the cryptic marks seemed to come alive, glowing with lunar radiance, and the observatory's energy enveloped him like a cosmic embrace.

As dawn broke and painted the horizon with hues of indigo and gold, Darius's meditation gradually came to an end, leaving him in the observatory's heart bathed in a soft, ethereal light. He knew that the Celestial Observatory had granted him a gift—the realisation that knowledge was not just a pursuit, but a dance of interconnected mysteries.

With the Cipher of Lunar Secrets in his hand and a spirit illuminated by the essence of cosmic wisdom, Darius returned to his city. He shared the tale of the "Celestial Observatory" and the revelations he had experienced with his fellow scholars and investigators, reminding them that the bond between seeker and universe was a dance of interconnected mysteries, and that the pursuit of cosmic insights was a symphony of discovery and unity.

And so, dear listener, the story of Darius and the "Celestial Observatory" teaches us that wisdom is a journey that transcends mere knowledge, that the bond between scholar and cosmos is a dance of interconnected mysteries, and that the essence of cosmic enlightenment is a timeless truth from the heart of ancient Persia.

The Starlit Labyrinth

Tracing Destiny's Threads Amidst the Constellations

In a land where nights were illuminated by stars that danced in the velvet sky, lived a young dreamer named Layla. Layla's eyes held the wonder of a stargazer, and her heart resonated with the mysteries of the cosmos.

One night, as Layla was tracing constellations with her fingers in the cool sand, an old sage with a staff adorned with celestial gems approached her. The sage's eyes held the brilliance of starlight, and his presence seemed to carry the echoes of celestial whispers. He observed Layla's stargazing with a knowing smile and said, "Your quest among the stars possesses the power to unveil destinies, but to truly understand the essence of fate, you must journey to the Starlit Labyrinth."

Intrigued by the sage's words, Layla expressed her interest in undertaking the journey. The sage nodded and handed her a small pendant that shimmered like a distant nebula. "Wear this Locket of Destiny, and let it guide your path," he said. "Seek the Starlit Labyrinth, where the paths of stars and the echoes of destinies intertwine."

With the Locket of Destiny around her neck and a heart brimming with anticipation, Layla set out on her journey to find the Starlit Labyrinth—a place spoken of in whispers, said to be a sanctuary where dreamers were not just observers, but weavers of the tapestry of fate. Guided by the shimmering constellations and the songs of the night breeze, she journeyed through moonlit valleys, crossed the river's reflection, and embraced the mysteries and revelations that her path held.

One night, as the stars painted the night sky with their cosmic brushstrokes and the heavens seemed to shimmer with secrets, Layla arrived at the entrance of the Starlit Labyrinth. The air was serene, yet alive with the faint hum of celestial harmonies. She noticed the labyrinth's entrance, adorned with patterns that seemed to shimmer like star trails.

As Layla stepped into the labyrinth's passage, she found herself surrounded by an ethereal aura—an ambiance that seemed to come from the very stars that adorned the sky. She held up the Locket of Destiny, and as the pendant caught the starlight, the labyrinth's atmosphere shifted, becoming a haven where celestial pathways and the threads of fate seemed to intertwine.

With a sense of reverence, Layla moved deeper into the labyrinth. She traced the intricate patterns that led to the heart of the maze, touched the luminous stones that held the echoes of countless journeys, and felt the presence of destinies intertwined with the very fabric of space.
As she moved among the labyrinth's wonders, she felt a connection—an interplay of energies that transcended the boundaries of earthly existence.

With the Locket of Destiny around her neck, Layla reached a central chamber—a place where the very essence of the Starlit Labyrinth seemed to converge. She gazed at the chamber and closed her eyes, allowing her thoughts to merge with the constellations above.
She felt a shift in the labyrinth's energy—the movements of stars, the alignments of planets, and the threads of destinies all seemed to harmonise into a symphony of interconnected fate.

With eyes closed and heart open to the symphony of cosmic destinies, Layla clasped the Locket of Destiny and let her fingers glide over its intricate design. As she did, a soft, celestial glow emanated from the locket, and the labyrinth's energy enveloped her like a celestial embrace.

As dawn broke and painted the horizon with hues of violet and gold, Layla's journey of contemplation gradually came to an end, leaving her in the labyrinth's heart bathed in a soft, ethereal light. She knew that the Starlit Labyrinth had granted her a gift—the realisation that fate was not just a path, but a dance of interconnected threads.

With the Locket of Destiny around her neck and a spirit illuminated by the essence of cosmic destinies, Layla returned to her home. She shared the tale of the "Starlit Labyrinth" and the revelations she had experienced with her fellow dreamers and stargazers, reminding them that the bond between seeker and stars was a dance of interconnected threads, and that the pursuit of destiny's patterns was a symphony of connection and unity.

And so, dear listener, the story of Layla and the "Starlit Labyrinth" teaches us that destiny is a journey that transcends mere pathways, that the bond between dreamer and cosmos is a dance of interconnected threads, and that the essence of fate's tapestry is a timeless trut from the heart of ancient Persia.

The Alchemical Arcana

Unveiling Mysteries in the Heart of Elemental Forces

In a realm where the arts of alchemy were practised as both science and magic, lived a young alchemist named Cyrus. Cyrus's eyes held the intensity of an experimenter, and his heart resonated with the enigma of transformation.

One day, as Cyrus was tending to his alchemical apparatus in a workshop filled with bubbling potions and intricate contraptions, an old sage with a staff adorned with elemental symbols approached him. The sage's eyes held the intensity of fire, the depth of water, the solidity of earth, and the whisper of air. His presence seemed to carry the echoes of secrets held by the elements themselves. He observed Cyrus's experiments with a knowing smile and said, "Your exploration of alchemical forces possesses the power to unveil elemental truths, but to truly understand the essence of creation, you must journey to the Arcane Nexus."

Intrigued by the sage's words, Cyrus expressed his interest in undertaking the journey. The sage nodded and handed him a small vial containing shimmering liquid. "Carry this Elixir of Elements with you, and let it guide your path," he said. "Seek the Arcane Nexus, where the energies of the elements and the echoes of creation intertwine."

With the Elixir of Elements in his hand and a heart brimming with curiosity, Cyrus set out on his journey to find the Arcane Nexus—a place spoken of in hushed tones, said to be a haven where alchemists were not just experimenters, but interpreters of the language of creation. Guided by the alignment of the stars and the whispers of alchemical winds, he journeyed through hidden caverns, crossed bridges over rushing rivers, and embraced the mysteries and revelations that his path held.

One night, as the moon's light filtered through ancient trees and the elements seemed to harmonise in a symphony of energy, Cyrus arrived at the entrance of the Arcane Nexus. The air was charged, yet serene, with an aura of ancient wisdom. He noticed the nexus's entrance, adorned with patterns that seemed to shimmer like arcane glyphs.

As Cyrus stepped into the nexus's centre, he found himself surrounded by an otherworldly aura—an ambiance that seemed to come from the very elements that composed the world. He held up the Elixir of

Elements, and as the liquid caught the moonlight, the nexus's energy shifted, becoming a sanctuary where the energies of creation and the mysteries of alchemy seemed to intertwine.

With a sense of reverence, Cyrus moved deeper into the nexus. He observed the central pedestal where the elemental forces seemed to converge, reached out to touch the delicate crystal formations that held the essence of fire, water, earth, and air, and felt the presence of ancient energies in the air. As he moved among the nexus's wonders, he felt a connection—an interplay of energies that transcended the boundaries of mere transformation.

With the Elixir of Elements in his hand, Cyrus approached the central pedestal—a focal point where the very essence of the Arcane Nexus seemed to converge. He gazed at the pedestal and closed his eyes, allowing his thoughts to merge with the elements around him. He felt a shift in the nexus's energy—the dance of flames, the flow of water, the stability of earth, and the whisper of air all seemed to harmonise into a symphony of interconnected creation.

With eyes closed and heart open to the symphony of alchemical energies, Cyrus uncorked the Elixir of Elements and let a drop fall onto the central pedestal. As the elixir merged with the crystal formations, a soft, ethereal glow spread through the nexus. In that moment of profound connection, he experienced a shift—the elements seemed to resonate, and the nexus's energy enveloped him like an embrace of pure creation.

As dawn broke and painted the horizon with hues of gold and amber, Cyrus's meditation gradually came to an end, leaving him in the nexus's heart bathed in a soft, otherworldly light. He knew that the Arcane Nexus had granted him a gift—the realisation that creation was not just a process, but a dance of interconnected energies.

With the Elixir of Elements in his hand and a spirit illuminated by the essence of alchemical forces, Cyrus returned to his workshop. He shared the tale of the "Arcane Nexus" and the revelations he had experienced with his fellow alchemists and experimenters, reminding them that the bond between creator and elements was a dance of interconnected energies, and that the pursuit of creation's mysteries was a symphony of understanding and unity.

And so, dear listener, the story of Cyrus and the "Arcane Nexus" teaches us that creation is a journey that transcends mere processes, that the bond between alchemist and elements is a dance of interconnected energies, and that the essence of alchemical wisdom is a timeless truth from the heart of ancient Persia.

The Veiled Tapestry

Threads of Destiny Woven in the Loom of Time

In a land where lush gardens bloomed with vibrant colours and fragrances, lived a young weaver named Lina. Lina's eyes held the perception of an artist, and her heart resonated with the beauty of creation.

One day, as Lina was crafting intricate patterns on a loom beneath the shade of flowering trees, an old sage with a staff adorned with woven symbols approached her. The sage's eyes held the depth of interwoven stories, and his presence seemed to carry the echoes of the past and future. He observed Lina's weaving with a knowing smile and said, "Your art of weaving possesses the power to unveil the stories of destiny, but to truly understand the essence of interconnectedness, you must journey to the Weaver's Sanctuary."

Intrigued by the sage's words, Lina expressed her interest in undertaking the journey. The sage nodded and handed her a small spindle that gleamed like a starlit night. "Carry this Spindle of Fate with you, and let it guide your path," he said. "Seek the Weaver's Sanctuary, where the threads of time and the echoes of stories intertwine."

With the Spindle of Fate in her hand and a heart brimming with anticipation, Lina set out on her journey to find the Weaver's Sanctuary—a place spoken of in whispers, said to be a haven where weavers were not just creators, but interpreters of the tapestry of life. Guided by the rustling leaves and the songs of birds, she journeyed through flower-filled meadows, crossed babbling brooks, and embraced the mysteries and revelations that her path held.

One evening, as the sun dipped below the horizon and the stars emerged to paint the sky with their luminous strokes, Lina arrived at the entrance of the Weaver's Sanctuary. The air was gentle, yet alive with the soft hum of weaving threads. She noticed the sanctuary's entrance, adorned with patterns that seemed to shimmer like woven tapestries.

As Lina stepped into the sanctuary's heart, she found herself surrounded by a serene aura—an ambiance that seemed to come from the very threads that adorned her loom. She held up the Spindle of Fate, and as its starlit surface caught the moonlight, the sanctuary's atmosphere shifted, becoming a haven where the art of weaving and the stories of time seemed to intertwine.

With a sense of reverence, Lina moved deeper into the sanctuary. She observed the looms that lined the walls like ancient storytellers, reached out to touch the vibrant threads that held the essence of countless moments, and felt the presence of destinies woven with the very fabric of existence.

As she moved among the sanctuary's wonders, she felt a connection—an interplay of energies that transcended the boundaries of mere creation.

With the Spindle of Fate in her hand, Lina approached a central loom—a masterpiece where the very essence of the Weaver's Sanctuary seemed to converge. She gazed at the loom and closed her eyes, allowing her thoughts to merge with the threads that surrounded her.

She felt a shift in the sanctuary's energy—the weavings of lives, the patterns of experiences, and the tales of destinies all seemed to harmonise into a symphony of interconnected stories.

With eyes closed and heart open to the symphony of woven narratives, Lina placed the Spindle of Fate onto the loom's surface. As she did, a soft, ethereal glow spread through the sanctuary, illuminating the threads in a dance of luminescence. In that moment of profound connection, she experienced a shift—the threads seemed to intertwine, and the sanctuary's energy enveloped her like a cocoon of intertwined stories.

As dawn broke and painted the horizon with hues of rose and gold, Lina's contemplation gradually came to an end, leaving her in the sanctuary's heart bathed in a soft, otherworldly light. She knew that the Weaver's Sanctuary had granted her a gift—the realisation that stories were not just narratives, but a dance of interconnected lives.

With the Spindle of Fate in her hand and a spirit illuminated by the essence of woven destinies, Lina returned to her garden. She shared the tale of the "Weaver's Sanctuary" and the revelations she had experienced with her fellow artists and creators, reminding them that the bond between weaver and tapestry was a dance of interconnected stories, and that the pursuit of understanding life's fabric was a symphony of empathy and unity.

And so, dear listener, the story of Lina and the "Weaver's Sanctuary" teaches us that life is a journey that transcends mere moments, that the bond between creator and creation is a dance of interconnected stories, and that the essence of understanding existence is a timeless truth from the heart of ancient Persia.

The Enchanted Oasis

Unveiling Magic in the Heart of the Desert

In a realm where vast deserts stretched under the scorching sun, there lay an oasis hidden from mortal eyes. It was said that within this oasis, the waters held the power to reveal hidden truths and grant glimpses of the future.

One day, a curious traveller named Farid embarked on a journey to find this elusive oasis. Guided by ancient maps and whispered legends, he ventured deep into the desert's embrace. His heart burned with the desire for knowledge and a thirst for the oasis's magic.

After days of arduous travel, Farid stumbled upon a lone palm tree, its leaves rustling mysteriously in the breeze. Intrigued, he followed the sound and soon found himself at the edge of an oasis, its waters shimmering like liquid crystal under the sun's rays.

With cautious steps, Farid knelt by the water's edge and gazed into its depths. He was mesmerised by the swirling patterns that seemed to form and dissolve within the liquid. As he peered closer, he saw fleeting images—a rider on a galloping horse, a city with soaring minarets, and a pair of intertwined serpents.

Eager to understand these visions, Farid dipped his hand into the water and splashed a few drops onto his face. The moment the droplets touched his skin, he was enveloped by a rush of sensations. His mind was flooded with fragments of stories and destinies intertwined, revealing secrets of distant lands and ages long past.

With each vision, Farid's understanding of the world expanded. He saw the rise and fall of empires, the struggles of heroes, and the quiet moments that shaped lives. As the sun dipped below the horizon, casting the desert in hues of orange and crimson, Farid felt a profound connection to the universe—the magic of the oasis had opened a window into the tapestry of existence.

As night blanketed the desert in starlight, Farid realised that the oasis's magic had granted him a gift—the ability to glimpse the threads of fate that wove through time itself. With gratitude in his heart, he whispered his thanks to the oasis and its waters, knowing that he would carry this newfound knowledge and perspective back to his people.

And so, dear listener, the tale of Farid and the "Enchanted Oasis" teaches us that the world holds hidden mysteries waiting to be uncovered, that the bond between seeker and magic is a dance of interconnected revelations, and that the essence of understanding existence is a timeless truth from the heart of ancient Persia.

The Whispering Winds

Seeking Guidance in the Songs of the Breeze

In the land of endless valleys and rolling hills, a young shepherd named Aria tended to her flock with care. Aria's eyes held the wisdom of the wild, and her heart resonated with the harmony of nature.

One evening, as the sun cast long shadows over the land, Aria noticed an unusual phenomenon—the wind seemed to carry whispers, each whisper holding a secret message. Curiosity piqued, she followed the wind's trail, climbing higher into the hills until she reached a secluded grove.

In the heart of the grove stood an ancient tree, its branches swaying in rhythm with the breeze. Aria approached the tree, and as she did, the whispers grew louder, forming words that spoke of hidden truths and paths yet untaken. The tree seemed to vibrate with energy, its leaves creating a symphony of guidance.

With reverence, Aria reached out and touched the tree's bark. She closed her eyes, allowing herself to be enveloped by the whispers. The wind's voice merged with her thoughts, revealing visions of distant lands and choices she would face. She saw a crossroads where paths diverged—an ancient city, a sunlit meadow, and a bustling marketplace.

As the night sky filled with stars, Aria understood that the whispers carried not only messages from the wind but also the wisdom of generations. The wind was a messenger of the ages, connecting her to the stories of those who had come before and those who would follow.

With gratitude in her heart, Aria thanked the tree and the wind for their guidance. She returned to her flock, carrying the knowledge that the harmony of nature held secrets waiting to be heard by those who listened. From that day on, she continued her shepherd's life with a newfound sense of purpose, knowing that the bond between seeker and nature was a dance of interconnected guidance.

And so, dear listener, the tale of Aria and the "Whispering Winds" teaches us that the world speaks to those who listen, that the bond between shepherd and wind is a dance of interconnected wisdom, and that the essence of understanding nature's secrets is a timeless truth from the heart of ancient Persia.

The Celestial Lute

Echoes of the Stars in a Melodious Journey

In a city where minarets touched the sky and marketplaces buzzed with life, there lived a young musician named Tarik. Tarik's eyes held the wonder of a dreamer, and his heart resonated with the melodies of the cosmos.

One night, as Tarik strummed his lute beneath a tapestry of stars, an old sage with a staff adorned with celestial symbols approached him. The sage's eyes held the radiance of constellations, and his presence seemed to carry the echoes of cosmic harmonies. He observed Tarik's music with a knowing smile and said, "Your melodies possess the power to unveil celestial secrets, but to truly understand the essence of the cosmos, you must journey to the Stellar Observatory."

Intrigued by the sage's words, Tarik expressed his interest in undertaking the journey. The sage nodded and handed him a small gem that sparkled like a distant star. "Carry this Starlit Gem with you, and let it guide your path," he said. "Seek the Stellar Observatory, where the songs of the stars and the echoes of melodies intertwine."

With the Starlit Gem in his hand and a heart brimming with anticipation, Tarik set out on his journey to find the Stellar Observatory—a place spoken of in whispers, said to be a sanctuary where musicians were not just performers, but interpreters of the celestial symphony. Guided by the twinkling constellations and the whispers of night winds, he journeyed through moonlit alleyways, passed by illuminated fountains, and embraced the mysteries and revelations that his path held.

One night, as the stars shone brightly in the indigo sky and the moon's glow bathed the city in silver light, Tarik arrived at the entrance of the Stellar Observatory. The air was still, yet alive with the cosmic hum of the universe. He noticed the observatory's entrance, adorned with patterns that seemed to shimmer like celestial notes.

As Tarik stepped into the observatory's chamber, he found himself surrounded by an ethereal aura—an ambiance that seemed to come from the very stars that adorned the night sky. He held up the Starlit Gem, and as it caught the moon's glow, the observatory's energy shifted, becoming a haven where celestial melodies and the mysteries of the cosmos seemed to intertwine.

With a sense of reverence, Tarik moved deeper into the observatory. He observed the celestial instruments that measured the rhythms of planets, reached out to touch the ethereal chimes that echoed cosmic vibrations, and felt the presence of celestial harmonies in the air.
As he moved among the observatory's wonders, he felt a connection—an interplay of energies that transcended the boundaries of earthly melodies.

With the Starlit Gem in his hand, Tarik approached a central platform—a stage where the very essence of the Stellar Observatory seemed to converge. He gazed at the platform and closed his eyes, allowing his thoughts to merge with the starlit expanse above.
He felt a shift in the observatory's energy—the twinkling of stars, the resonance of galaxies, and the echoes of celestial music all seemed to harmonise into a symphony of interconnected melodies.

With eyes closed and heart open to the symphony of cosmic harmonies, Tarik held the Starlit Gem to his heart and let his fingers dance over his lute's strings. As he played, the gem's radiance seemed to intensify, and the observatory's energy enveloped him like a cosmic embrace.

As dawn broke and painted the horizon with hues of pink and gold, Tarik's music gradually came to an end, leaving him in the observatory's heart bathed in a soft, otherworldly light. He knew that the Stellar Observatory had granted him a gift—the realisation that melodies were not just sounds, but a dance of interconnected harmonies.

With the Starlit Gem in his hand and a spirit illuminated by the essence of cosmic melodies, Tarik returned to his city. He shared the tale of the "Stellar Observatory" and the revelations he had experienced with his fellow musicians and dreamers, reminding them that the bond between musician and cosmos was a dance of interconnected harmonies, and that the pursuit of cosmic melodies was a symphony of connection and unity.

And so, dear listener, the story of Tarik and the "Stellar Observatory" teaches us that music is a journey that transcends mere notes, that the bond between musician and stars is a dance of interconnected harmonies, and that the essence of cosmic resonance is a timeless truth from the heart of ancient Persia.

The Labyrinth of Dreams

Exploring the Realms of Imagination and Reality

In a realm where dreams and reality were intertwined, a young dreamer named Nadia roamed the landscapes of both the waking world and the realm of slumber. Nadia's eyes held the sparkle of endless possibilities, and her heart resonated with the magic of imagination.

One night, as the moon cast its silvery glow over the world, Nadia ventured into a forest known for its ethereal properties. Among the trees, she discovered an ancient, overgrown labyrinth—the Labyrinth of Dreams. It was said that those who entered the labyrinth could explore the realm of dreams in all its forms.

Intrigued by the labyrinth's mysteries, Nadia entered its twisting passages. As she walked, she found herself transported into a dreamscape where reality and imagination intertwined.
She walked through enchanted gardens that bloomed with vibrant colours, soared through starlit skies on the back of a mythical creature, and even conversed with talking animals that shared ancient wisdom.

With each step, Nadia's understanding of the world expanded. She experienced the magic of transformation, the power of creation, and the profound interconnectedness of all things. She realised that within the Labyrinth of Dreams, the boundaries between the waking world and the realm of slumber were blurred—a testament to the limitless potential of human imagination.

As the night deepened and the moon reached its zenith, Nadia encountered a central chamber within the labyrinth. In this chamber, a luminous pool reflected the starry sky above and the dreamscape below. Nadia gazed into the pool, and as she did, the reflections seemed to dance and shift, showing glimpses of forgotten memories and untold stories.

With wonder in her heart, Nadia extended her hand to touch the pool's surface. The moment her fingertips made contact, she felt a rush of emotions—a kaleidoscope of experiences that belonged to countless dreamers and storytellers throughout time. She realised that the Labyrinth of Dreams was not merely a place of exploration—it was a repository of the collective imagination, a tapestry woven from the threads of countless minds.

With gratitude for the labyrinth's revelations, Nadia thanked the dream realm and the labyrinth itself for its wisdom. She emerged from the labyrinth, carrying with her the knowledge that the bond between dreamer and reality was a dance of interconnected experiences.
From that day on, she lived her life with a renewed sense of wonder, knowing that the realm of dreams held secrets waiting to be unlocked by those who dared to venture into the Labyrinth of Dreams.

And so, dear listener, the tale of Nadia and the "Labyrinth of Dreams" teaches us that the boundaries between reality and imagination are fluid, that the bond between dreamer and dreamscape is a dance of interconnected experiences, and that the essence of exploring the realms of possibility is a timeless truth from the heart of ancient Persia.

The Sands of Remembrance

Unearthing Echoes of the Past in the Desert's Embrace

In a land where ancient ruins lay buried beneath the shifting sands, lived a young archaeologist named Zara. Zara's eyes held the curiosity of a seeker, and her heart resonated with the mysteries of history.

One day, as Zara explored the ruins of an abandoned city, she uncovered a hidden chamber beneath layers of earth and debris. In the heart of the chamber stood a weathered stone tablet adorned with intricate symbols—a key to unlocking the secrets of the past.

With careful hands, Zara deciphered the symbols and learned of a forgotten ritual—the Ritual of Sands. It was said that by performing this ritual at the heart of the desert, one could connect with the memories of ancient civilizations and unveil the stories they left behind.

Intrigued by the tablet's revelations, Zara gathered her tools and set out for the heart of the desert. Guided by her knowledge and the alignment of the stars, she journeyed through sand dunes and wind-sculpted rocks, embracing the solitude of the desert's embrace.

As the sun cast long shadows across the desert landscape, Zara arrived at the designated location—an oasis surrounded by towering dunes. With the stone tablet in hand, she followed the instructions, drawing intricate patterns in the sand and invoking the ancient incantations.

With each movement, Zara felt a connection to the sands beneath her feet and the stories they held. A soft breeze whispered secrets carried by generations, and the air seemed to shimmer with the echoes of forgotten voices. Zara closed her eyes, allowing herself to become one with the desert—a vessel through which the memories of civilizations past could flow.

As night draped the desert in a blanket of stars, Zara's senses expanded. She saw visions of bustling marketplaces, towering palaces, and the faces of people who had once walked the same sands. She felt their triumphs and struggles, their joys and sorrows, all woven into the tapestry of time.

With each revelation, Zara's understanding of history deepened. She realised that the desert was not merely a barren expanse—it was a repository of memories, a library of the past waiting to be unearthed. The Ritual of Sands had granted her the gift of connecting with the stories etched into the very land.

With gratitude in her heart, Zara completed the ritual and thanked the desert for its revelations. She returned to her city, carrying with her the knowledge that the bond between seeker and history was a dance of interconnected stories.

From that day on, she continued her archaeological pursuits with a renewed sense of purpose, knowing that the sands of the desert held secrets waiting to be discovered by those who were willing to listen. And so, dear listener, the story of Zara and the "Sands of Remembrance" teaches us that history is a journey that transcends time, that the bond between archaeologist and past is a dance of interconnected stories, and that the essence of unearthing the echoes of the past is a timeless truth from the heart of ancient Persia.

The Oracle's Gaze

Seeking Guidance in the Reflections of Destiny

In a land where temples adorned with golden domes graced the landscape, a young seer named Kasra held the gift of second sight. Kasra's eyes held the depth of a visionary, and his heart resonated with the mysteries of fate.

One evening, as the sun dipped below the horizon and the sky blazed with hues of crimson and gold, Kasra received a vision—a vision of a distant lake known as the Oracle's Mirror. It was said that the waters of this lake held the power to reveal glimpses of the future and offer guidance to those who sought it.

Intrigued by the vision, Kasra embarked on a journey to find the Oracle's Mirror. Guided by his inner sense and the whispers of his visions, he travelled through valleys and climbed rugged mountains until he reached the lake's shores—a tranquil oasis surrounded by lush foliage.

As Kasra gazed into the waters, he saw ripples forming intricate patterns—a dance of reflections that seemed to unveil the stories of lives yet to be lived. He saw faces of people he had never met, places he had never visited, and moments that shimmered like stars in the fabric of time.

With each ripple, Kasra's understanding of the world expanded. He witnessed the ebb and flow of destinies, the choices that shaped lives, and the interconnectedness of all beings. He realised that within the Oracle's Mirror, the boundaries between the present and the future were blurred—a testament to the enigmatic nature of destiny.

As night draped the landscape in a cloak of darkness, Kasra's visions grew more vivid. He saw pivotal moments—crossroads where paths converged, decisions that had the power to alter the course of history, and the echoes of actions that rippled through time.

With each revelation, Kasra's heart swelled with a profound sense of purpose. He understood that the Oracle's Mirror was not merely a pool of water—it was a gateway to the realm of possibilities, a portal through which the future could be glimpsed and understood.

With gratitude in his heart, Kasra thanked the Oracle's Mirror and the lake itself for its guidance. He returned to his temple, carrying with him the knowledge that the bond between seer and destiny was a dance of interconnected paths. From that day on, he shared his insights with those who sought his guidance, knowing that the Oracle's Mirror held secrets waiting to be revealed to those who dared to peer into its depths.

And so, dear listener, the tale of Kasra and the "Oracle's Gaze" teaches us that the future is a journey that transcends the present, that the bond between seer and destiny is a dance of interconnected visions, and that the essence of seeking guidance in reflections is a timeless truth from the heart of ancient Persia.

The Enchanted Scribe

Unlocking Wisdom in the Pages of an Ancient Scroll

In a city where scholars congregated and libraries held treasures of knowledge, lived a young scribe named Leyla. Leyla's eyes held the curiosity of a learner, and her heart resonated with the wisdom of ages.

One day, as Leyla was cataloguing ancient manuscripts, she came across a scroll adorned with intricate symbols—an artefact said to hold the secrets of forgotten languages. As she traced her fingers over the symbols, they seemed to glow with an otherworldly light.

Intrigued by the scroll's mysteries, Leyla embarked on a quest to decipher its contents. Guided by the guidance of celestial alignments and the teachings of her mentors, she journeyed through the corridors of knowledge and across sunlit courtyards, embracing the journey that the scroll's symbols promised.

As the sun's rays filtered through the windows of the grand library, Leyla finally deciphered the symbols, unveiling a series of incantations—a key to unlocking the scroll's enchantment. With the incantations in her heart and the scroll in her hand, she recited the words, and as she did, the scroll's energy transformed into a portal—a gateway to the realm of ancient wisdom.

With a sense of reverence, Leyla stepped through the portal and found herself in an ethereal realm where the boundaries between the physical and the metaphysical were blurred. She encountered luminous beings who spoke in riddles and shared insights that transcended time. They revealed tales of forgotten civilizations, explained the mysteries of the cosmos, and delved into the nature of existence itself.

With each encounter, Leyla's understanding of the world expanded. She saw the tapestry of history woven with threads of truth and legend, and she felt the interconnectedness of all things—past, present, and future. She realised that within the realm of the Enchanted Scribe, the boundaries between mundane reality and the realms of imagination were dissolved—a testament to the boundless potential of human inquiry.

As the realm's luminous beings gradually faded into the background, Leyla knew that the Enchanted Scribe had granted her a gift—the ability to connect with the wisdom of ages, to seek knowledge beyond the limitations of her time.

With gratitude in her heart, Leyla stepped back through the portal, returning to the grand library with the scroll and its revelations.
She shared the tale of her journey with her fellow scholars and seekers, reminding them that the bond between scribe and wisdom was a dance of interconnected insights, and that the pursuit of understanding was a symphony of exploration and unity.

And so, dear listener, the story of Leyla and the "Enchanted Scribe" teaches us that knowledge is a journey that transcends the boundaries of time, that the bond between seeker and wisdom is a dance of interconnected insights, and that the essence of unlocking ancient truths is a timeless truth from the heart of ancient Persia.

The Radiant Loom

Weaving Stories of Light in the Fabric of Reality

In a land where sun-kissed plains stretched beneath the open sky, lived a young weaver named Amir. Amir's eyes held the creativity of an artist, and his heart resonated with the magic of creation.

One day, as Amir wove intricate patterns on his loom, he received a vision—a vision of a legendary loom known as the Radiant Loom. It was said that within the threads of this loom, the power of sunlight was woven into dazzling tapestries that held the stories of the land.

Intrigued by the vision, Amir set out to find the Radiant Loom. Guided by his intuition and the whispers of wind, he journeyed through fields of wildflowers and under the shade of ancient trees, embracing the beauty that surrounded him.

After days of travel, Amir arrived at a meadow aglow with sunlight. In the centre stood the Radiant Loom, its threads glistening with an otherworldly brilliance. Amir approached the loom, and as he did, the threads seemed to come to life, dancing in the sunlight's embrace.

With reverence, Amir sat before the loom and picked up a golden thread. He began to weave, allowing his fingers to be guided by the magic of the moment. With each movement, the thread transformed, shimmering with hues of red, orange, and gold. He saw images forming—scenes of nature's beauty, tales of heroes and adventurers, and the essence of life's vibrant journey.

As the sun dipped below the horizon and the sky was painted with a tapestry of colours, Amir's weaving took on a life of its own. The Radiant Loom's magic seemed to amplify his creative energy, and the threads wove stories that resonated with the heartbeats of the land.

With each tapestry, Amir's understanding of the world expanded. He realised that the Radiant Loom was not merely a tool—it was a conduit through which the stories of the land were woven into existence. He understood that the bond between creator and creation was a dance of interconnected energies—a symphony of light and creativity.

As dawn broke and painted the horizon with hues of pink and gold, Amir's weaving gradually came to an end, leaving him in the meadow's embrace bathed in a soft, otherworldly light.

He knew that the Radiant Loom had granted him a gift—the ability to weave stories that were not just narratives, but reflections of the world's beauty and wonder.

With gratitude in his heart, Amir returned to his village, carrying with him the tapestries and their revelations. He shared the tale of the "Radiant Loom" and the insights he had gained with his fellow weavers and artists, reminding them that the bond between creator and creation was a dance of interconnected energies, and that the pursuit of beauty and creativity was a symphony of expression and unity.

And so, dear listener, the story of Amir and the "Radiant Loom" teaches us that creativity is a journey that transcends artistic boundaries, that the bond between weaver and tapestry is a dance of interconnected energies, and that the essence of weaving stories of light is a timeless truth from the heart of ancient Persia.

The Oasis Oracle

Unveiling Prophecies in the Ripples of Still Waters

In a desert where dunes stretched to the horizon and oases were coveted like gems, lived a young nomad named Farah. Farah's eyes held the depth of a seeker, and her heart resonated with the mysteries of destiny.

One day, as Farah rested beside an oasis, she noticed a peculiar phenomenon—the water's surface seemed to shimmer with reflections that formed intricate patterns. It was said that within the ripples of the oasis, the power of divination was hidden, and those who gazed into its depths could glimpse glimpses of the future.

Intrigued by the oasis's mysteries, Farah decided to seek its prophecies. Guided by the alignments of stars and the whispers of desert winds, she journeyed across the sands, embracing the solitude of the desert's embrace and the wisdom that it promised.

As the sun cast its golden light across the landscape, Farah arrived at the oasis's edge—a haven of still waters surrounded by verdant palms. With a sense of anticipation, she knelt by the water's edge and gazed into its depths. The ripples seemed to dance and shift, forming intricate patterns that held the stories of lives yet to unfold.

With each ripple, Farah's understanding of the world expanded. She saw glimpses of pivotal moments—crossroads where destinies converged, decisions that carried weight, and the echoes of actions that rippled through time. She felt the interconnectedness of all things, the way each choice and consequence wove together into the fabric of existence.

As the stars emerged in the indigo sky and the desert embraced the night, Farah's visions grew more vivid. She saw faces of people she had never met, landscapes she had never visited, and the dance of events that unfolded like constellations in the sky.

With each revelation, Farah's heart filled with a profound sense of purpose. She understood that the Oasis Oracle was not merely a pool of water—it was a mirror of destiny, a gateway to the realm of possibilities, and a reflection of the tapestry of existence itself.

With gratitude in her heart, Farah thanked the oasis and its prophecies. She returned to her nomadic life, carrying with her the knowledge that the bond between seeker and destiny was a dance of interconnected stories.

From that day on, she lived her life with a renewed sense of wonder, knowing that the oasis's waters held secrets waiting to be glimpsed by those who dared to gaze into their depths.

And so, dear listener, the tale of Farah and the "Oasis Oracle" teaches us that destiny is a journey that transcends the present moment, that the bond between seeker and prophecy is a dance of interconnected stories, and that the essence of unveiling glimpses of the future is a timeless truth from the heart of ancient Persia.

The Celestial Navigator

Guiding Ships Through the Stars of Destiny

In a coastal town where waves kissed the shores and ships set sail under the vast sky, lived a young sailor named Ramin. Ramin's eyes held the wonder of an explorer, and his heart resonated with the mysteries of the cosmos.

One evening, as Ramin looked up at the starry night, he received a vision—a vision of a celestial instrument known as the Celestial Navigator. It was said that within the Navigator's intricate gears, the power to chart paths through the stars was hidden, and those who understood its secrets could navigate their ships through the tapestry of constellations.

Intrigued by the vision, Ramin set out to find the Celestial Navigator. Guided by his intuition and the ancient star maps, he journeyed through coastal towns and under the watchful eyes of seagulls, embracing the journey that the Navigator's gears promised.

After days of travel, Ramin arrived at a weathered observatory perched on a cliff overlooking the sea. In its heart stood the Celestial Navigator—a masterpiece of gears and lenses that seemed to capture the very essence of the night sky. Ramin approached the Navigator, and as he did, its gears began to turn, aligning with the celestial patterns above.

With reverence, Ramin took hold of the Navigator's handles and began to chart the stars' positions. As he turned the gears, the constellations seemed to come to life, forming intricate patterns that held the secrets of the night sky. He saw the Milky Way stretching across the heavens, the North Star guiding its steady course, and the constellations that had guided sailors for generations.

As the moon cast its silvery glow over the observatory, Ramin's navigation took on a life of its own. The Celestial Navigator's magic seemed to amplify his understanding of the stars, and the constellations revealed their stories and the interconnectedness of the cosmos.

With each celestial chart, Ramin's understanding of the world expanded. He realised that the Celestial Navigator was not merely a tool—it was a conduit through which the stories of the stars were unveiled. He understood that the bond between navigator and stars was a dance of interconnected energies—a symphony of celestial patterns and exploration.

As dawn broke and painted the horizon with hues of rose and gold, Ramin's navigation gradually came to an end, leaving him in the observatory's embrace bathed in a soft, otherworldly light. He knew that the Celestial Navigator had granted him a gift—the ability to chart not only the paths of ships but the threads of the universe itself.

With gratitude in his heart, Ramin returned to his coastal town, carrying with him the celestial charts and their revelations. He shared the tale of the "Celestial Navigator" and the insights he had gained with his fellow sailors and dreamers, reminding them that the bond between navigator and stars was a dance of interconnected energies, and that the pursuit of exploration and understanding was a symphony of discovery and unity.

And so, dear listener, the story of Ramin and the "Celestial Navigator" teaches us that exploration is a journey that transcends earthly horizons, that the bond between sailor and stars is a dance of interconnected energies, and that the essence of charting paths through the cosmos is a timeless truth from the heart of ancient Persia.

The Dreamer's Sanctuary

Unveiling Truths in the Land of Slumber

In a land where starlight painted the night sky and dreams held the promise of hidden revelations, lived a young dreamer named Soraya. Soraya's eyes held the wonder of a seeker, and her heart resonated with the mysteries of the subconscious.

One night, as Soraya closed her eyes and surrendered to the realm of slumber, she found herself in a dreamscape unlike any other—a sanctuary where the boundaries between reality and imagination were blurred. It was said that within the Dreamer's Sanctuary, the power to unveil truths and unravel mysteries of the mind was hidden.

Intrigued by the dreamscape's mysteries, Soraya ventured deeper into the sanctuary. As she walked, she encountered enigmatic figures who seemed to dance on the edge of consciousness, sharing cryptic messages and tales that resonated with her very being.

Guided by her intuition and the luminescent pathways, Soraya journeyed through ethereal landscapes—forests of shifting colours, rivers of memories, and mountains of reflection. She saw doorways that led to forgotten moments and mirrors that revealed the layers of her identity.

With each step, Soraya's understanding of the world expanded. She witnessed the interplay of emotions, the tapestry of experiences that shaped her reality, and the threads of possibility woven into the fabric of her existence. She realised that within the Dreamer's Sanctuary, the boundaries between dreams and waking life were dissolved—a testament to the fluidity of perception.

As the moon cast its silvery glow over the dreamscape, Soraya's visions grew more vivid. She saw echoes of choices and actions that had shaped her path, and she felt the interconnectedness of her journey with the lives of others.

With each revelation, Soraya's heart swelled with a profound sense of self-awareness. She understood that the Dreamer's Sanctuary was not merely a realm of slumber—it was a portal to the realm of the subconscious, a mirror that reflected the truths hidden within her soul.

As dawn's light began to pierce the horizon, Soraya's dream journey gradually came to an end, leaving her in the Dreamer's Sanctuary's embrace bathed in a soft, otherworldly light. She knew that the sanctuary had granted her a gift—the ability to explore not only her dreams but the depths of her own mind.

With gratitude in her heart, Soraya awoke from her dream and carried with her the insights and revelations she had gained.

She shared the tale of the "Dreamer's Sanctuary" and the wisdom she had discovered with her fellow dreamers and seekers, reminding them that the bond between dreamer and dreamscape was a dance of interconnected perceptions, and that the pursuit of self-discovery and understanding was a symphony of introspection and unity.

And so, dear listener, the story of Soraya and the "Dreamer's Sanctuary" teaches us that self-discovery is a journey that transcends waking life, that the bond between dreamer and dreamscape is a dance of interconnected perceptions, and that the essence of unveiling hidden truths is a timeless truth from the heart of ancient Persia.

The Whispering Grove

Discovering Secrets in the Heart of an Enchanted Forest

In a realm where lush forests whispered ancient secrets and creatures of myth roamed free, lived a young explorer named Darius. Darius's eyes held the wonder of a wanderer, and his heart resonated with the mysteries of nature.

One day, as Darius ventured into an uncharted forest, he stumbled upon a grove unlike any other—a grove where the trees seemed to murmur in a language only he could understand. It was said that within the Whispering Grove, the power to commune with nature's spirits and uncover hidden knowledge was hidden.

Intrigued by the grove's mysteries, Darius entered its heart. As he walked among the ancient trees, he felt the rustling leaves and heard the gentle whispers that seemed to carry tales of forgotten times. He listened with an open heart, allowing the forest's voice to guide him deeper into the realm of nature's magic.

Guided by the melodies of the wind and the patterns of light filtering through the canopy, Darius journeyed through the grove's enchanting pathways—streams that sparkled like stars, clearings where moonlight danced, and stone arches carved with ancient symbols.

With each step, Darius's understanding of the world expanded. He learned the language of the birds, the stories of the creatures that called the forest home, and the symbiotic dance of life and balance that played out in nature's embrace. He realised that within the Whispering Grove, the boundaries between human and nature were blurred—a testament to the interconnectedness of all living things.

As night draped the grove in a blanket of starlight, Darius's communion with the forest grew more profound. He felt the rhythms of the earth beneath his feet, saw visions of nature's wonders, and understood the ancient truths whispered by the trees themselves.

With each revelation, Darius's heart filled with a profound sense of harmony. He knew that the Whispering Grove was not merely a collection of trees—it was a living testament to the unity of all things, a realm where humans and nature danced in perfect synchrony.

As dawn's light painted the horizon with hues of gold and amber, Darius's exploration gradually came to an end, leaving him in the heart of the Whispering Grove bathed in a soft, otherworldly glow. He knew that the grove had granted him a gift—the ability to commune with nature's spirits and uncover the secrets woven into the fabric of existence.

With gratitude in his heart, Darius left the grove and returned to his village, carrying with him the insights and wisdom he had gained. He shared the tale of the "Whispering Grove" and the revelations of his journey with his fellow explorers and nature enthusiasts, reminding them that the bond between seeker and nature was a dance of interconnected whispers, and that the pursuit of harmony and understanding was a symphony of communion and unity.

And so, dear listener, the story of Darius and the "Whispering Grove" teaches us that nature is a journey that transcends human comprehension, that the bond between explorer and forest is a dance of interconnected whispers, and that the essence of uncovering hidden knowledge is a timeless truth from the heart of ancient Persia.

The Starweaver's Legacy

Spinning Cosmic Tales in the Threads of the Night Sky

In a land where the night sky blazed with constellations and tales of the cosmos were told through the ages, lived a young storyteller named Layla. Layla's eyes held the depth of a dreamer, and her heart resonated with the mysteries of the universe.

One evening, as Layla sat under a star-studded sky, she received a vision—a vision of a legendary weaver known as the Starweaver. It was said that within the threads of the Starweaver's loom, the power to craft tales of the cosmos was hidden, and those who understood its secrets could spin stories that connected humanity to the stars.

Intrigued by the vision, Layla embarked on a quest to find the Starweaver's Legacy. Guided by the patterns of the constellations and the echoes of ancient stories, she journeyed through open fields and along moonlit paths, embracing the journey that the Starweaver's loom promised.

After days of travel, Layla arrived at a hilltop where an observatory stood—a place of quiet reverence that overlooked the world and the heavens above. In its centre stood the Starweaver's Legacy—a loom adorned with celestial patterns that seemed to capture the essence of the night sky. Layla approached the loom, and as she did, its threads began to shimmer with an ethereal light.

With reverence, Layla sat before the loom and picked up a thread that sparkled like stardust. She began to weave, allowing her fingers to be guided by the magic of the cosmos. With each movement, the thread transformed, taking on hues of blue, silver, and gold. She saw images forming—scenes of celestial wonders, tales of heroes among the stars, and the journey of humanity's connection to the cosmos.

As the constellations shifted in the sky and the moon's radiance bathed the observatory, Layla's storytelling took on a life of its own. The Starweaver's Legacy's magic seemed to amplify her creativity, and the threads wove tales that resonated with the heartbeats of the universe.

With each woven tapestry, Layla's understanding of the world expanded. She realised that the Starweaver's Legacy was not merely a tool—it was a gateway through which the stories of the cosmos were told. She understood that the bond between storyteller and universe was a dance of interconnected energies—a symphony of imagination and cosmic exploration.

As the night's tapestry deepened, Layla's storytelling gradually came to an end, leaving her in the observatory's embrace bathed in a soft, otherworldly light. She knew that the Starweaver's Legacy had granted her a gift—the ability to connect not only with humanity's tales but with the stories of the stars themselves.

With gratitude in her heart, Layla returned to her village, carrying with her the woven tapestries and the wisdom they contained.
She shared the tale of the "Starweaver's Legacy" and the insights she had gained with her fellow storytellers and stargazers, reminding them that the bond between weaver and universe was a dance of interconnected energies, and that the pursuit of cosmic storytelling and understanding was a symphony of wonder and unity.

And so, dear listener, the story of Layla and the "Starweaver's Legacy" teaches us that the universe is a journey that transcends earthly horizons, that the bond between storyteller and cosmos is a dance of interconnected energies, and that the essence of spinning tales of the night sky is a timeless truth from the heart of ancient Persia.

The Arcane Alchemist

Unlocking Mysteries in the Elixirs of Transformation

In a city where marketplaces bustled with traders and hidden alleys whispered of secrets, lived a young alchemist named Arash. Arash's eyes held the curiosity of a seeker, and his heart resonated with the mysteries of transformation.

One day, as Arash experimented with alchemical concoctions in his laboratory, he received a vision—a vision of an ancient alchemical tome known as the Arcane Codex. It was said that within the pages of the Codex, the power to unlock the secrets of elemental transformation was hidden, and those who deciphered its teachings could harness the forces of nature.

Intrigued by the vision, Arash set out to find the Arcane Codex. Guided by the alignments of stars and the whispers of his mentors, he journeyed through bustling bazaars and quiet corners, embracing the journey that the Codex's pages promised.

After days of travel, Arash arrived at an ancient library tucked away in a forgotten part of the city—a repository of knowledge and wisdom. In its heart stood the Arcane Codex—a book adorned with intricate symbols that seemed to shimmer with an otherworldly light.
Arash opened the Codex, and as he did, its pages seemed to come alive, revealing alchemical formulas and arcane secrets.

With reverence, Arash delved into the Codex's teachings, immersing himself in the alchemical arts. He mixed rare herbs, captured the essence of celestial elements, and conducted experiments that seemed to defy the laws of nature. He saw the colours of transformation—the albedo, the rubedo, and the nigredo—unfolding before his eyes.

As the moon cast its glow over the laboratory and the air crackled with energy, Arash's experiments took on a life of their own. The Arcane Codex's magic seemed to amplify his understanding of alchemy, and the elixirs he crafted revealed the dance of elements and the mysteries of transformation.

With each elixir, Arash's understanding of the world expanded. He realised that the Arcane Codex was not merely a collection of pages—it was a portal through which the mysteries of elemental forces were unveiled. He understood that the bond between alchemist and nature was a dance of interconnected energies—a symphony of discovery and metamorphosis.

As the laboratory's flames danced and the night deepened, Arash's experiments gradually came to an end, leaving him in the embrace of the alchemical mysteries bathed in a soft, otherworldly glow. He knew that the Arcane Codex had granted him a gift—the ability to understand not only the physical world but the hidden forces that shaped it.

With gratitude in his heart, Arash left the library and returned to his laboratory, carrying with him the elixirs and their revelations.

He shared the tale of the "Arcane Alchemist" and the insights he had gained with his fellow alchemists and seekers of wisdom, reminding them that the bond between seeker and knowledge was a dance of interconnected energies, and that the pursuit of transformation and understanding was a symphony of experimentation and unity.

And so, dear listener, the story of Arash and the "Arcane Alchemist" teaches us that transformation is a journey that transcends the boundaries of matter, that the bond between alchemist and knowledge is a dance of interconnected energies, and that the essence of unlocking mysteries in elixirs is a timeless truth from the heart of ancient Persia.

The Echoing Minaret

Unveiling the Threads of History in a Tower of Stories

In a city where minarets punctuated the skyline and tales of generations echoed through narrow streets, lived a young historian named Nasrin. Nasrin's eyes held the depth of a time traveller, and her heart resonated with the mysteries of the past.

One day, as Nasrin explored an ancient mosque, she heard whispers in the wind—a chorus of voices that seemed to carry the stories of centuries. It was said that within the Echoing Minaret, the power to connect with the echoes of history and unveil forgotten narratives was hidden.

Intrigued by the whispers, Nasrin ascended the minaret's spiral staircase. As she climbed higher, the echoes grew stronger, and she felt the weight of generations past. Guided by the cadence of voices and the imprints of time, she journeyed through the minaret's chambers and passages, embracing the stories that awaited her.

With each step, Nasrin's understanding of the world expanded. She heard the tales of scholars who had debated beneath the minaret's arches, the prayers of the faithful that had echoed through its halls, and the whispers of lovers who had sought solace within its walls. She felt the interconnectedness of all those who had passed through—a testament to the timeless nature of human experience.

As the sun cast its golden light over the city and the minaret's shadow stretched across the landscape, Nasrin reached the summit—a platform that offered a panoramic view of the world below. There, she closed her eyes and listened to the echoes that danced in the breeze, revealing fragments of lives and stories that had shaped the city's history.

With each whispered narrative, Nasrin's heart swelled with a profound sense of empathy. She understood that the Echoing Minaret was not merely a tower—it was a vessel through which the voices of the past could be heard. She realised that the bond between historian and history was a dance of interconnected narratives—a symphony of remembrance and storytelling.

As twilight painted the sky with hues of purple and gold, Nasrin's connection with the minaret's echoes gradually came to an end, leaving her on the platform bathed in a soft, otherworldly light. She knew that the minaret had granted her a gift—the ability to connect not only with the present but with the threads of history itself.

With gratitude in her heart, Nasrin descended the minaret and returned to her city, carrying with her the stories and echoes she had encountered. She shared the tale of the "Echoing Minaret" and the insights she had gained with her fellow historians and seekers of truth, reminding them that the bond between seeker and history was a dance of interconnected narratives, and that the pursuit of understanding and remembrance was a symphony of connection and unity.

And so, dear listener, the story of Nasrin and the "Echoing Minaret" teaches us that history is a journey that transcends the boundaries of time, that the bond between historian and echoes is a dance of interconnected narratives, and that the essence of unveiling forgotten stories is a timeless truth from the heart of ancient Persia.

The Labyrinth of Echoes

Unravelling Secrets in the Heart of a Mysterious Maze

In a kingdom where palaces stood in the shadows of towering mountains, lived a young explorer named Tariq. Tariq's eyes held the curiosity of a puzzle solver, and his heart resonated with the mysteries of hidden paths.

One day, as Tariq ventured into a remote valley, he discovered an entrance to a labyrinth unlike any other—a labyrinth where every twist and turn seemed to echo with cryptic whispers. It was said that within the Labyrinth of Echoes, the power to unravel enigmas and discover hidden truths was hidden.

Intrigued by the labyrinth's mysteries, Tariq stepped inside. As he navigated its passages, he heard the echoing footfalls and caught fleeting glimpses of shadows that seemed to move just beyond his vision. Guided by the echoes and his intuition, he journeyed through the labyrinth's intricate pathways—chambers of reflection, corridors of riddles, and intersections that held the promise of revelation.

With each step, Tariq's understanding of the world expanded. He deciphered cryptic inscriptions that adorned the walls, solved puzzles that seemed to defy logic, and followed the echoes that led him deeper into the realm of enigma. He realised that within the Labyrinth of Echoes, the boundaries between reality and illusion were blurred—a testament to the interconnectedness of perception and truth.

As the moon's glow illuminated the labyrinth's passages and the air hummed with mystery, Tariq's journey grew more profound. He encountered statues that seemed to come to life, doorways that opened to unforeseen realms, and mirrors that reflected not only his image but the echoes of forgotten ages.

With each enigma unravelled, Tariq's heart swelled with a profound sense of revelation. He knew that the Labyrinth of Echoes was not merely a maze—it was a repository of hidden knowledge, a realm where seekers of truth could unveil the stories that had shaped its existence.

As dawn's light began to paint the labyrinth's walls with hues of gold and rose, Tariq's exploration gradually came to an end, leaving him at the heart of the labyrinth bathed in a soft, otherworldly glow. He knew that the labyrinth had granted him a gift—the ability to unravel not only the puzzles of the maze but the enigmas of life itself.

With gratitude in his heart, Tariq emerged from the labyrinth and returned to his kingdom, carrying with him the insights and revelations he had gained.

He shared the tale of the "Labyrinth of Echoes" and the wisdom of his journey with his fellow explorers and puzzle solvers, reminding them that the bond between seeker and enigma was a dance of interconnected echoes, and that the pursuit of uncovering hidden truths and understanding was a symphony of curiosity and unity.

And so, dear listener, the story of Tariq and the "Labyrinth of Echoes" teaches us that enigma is a journey that transcends the boundaries of logic, that the bond between explorer and mystery is a dance of interconnected echoes, and that the essence of unravelling secrets is a timeless truth from the heart of ancient Persia.

The Celestial Weaver

Creating Destinies in the Constellations of the Night Sky

In a land where the night sky was a canvas of stars and legends of destiny adorned the tapestries of time, lived a young artist named Leyla. Leyla's eyes held the vision of a dreamer, and her heart resonated with the mysteries of fate.

One night, as Leyla gazed up at the celestial expanse, she received a vision—a vision of a legendary weaver known as the Celestial Weaver. It was said that within the patterns of the night sky, the power to shape destinies and weave the threads of life was hidden, and those who understood its secrets could create narratives that guided humanity's journey.

Intrigued by the vision, Leyla set out to find the Celestial Weaver's Wisdom. Guided by the alignment of stars and the whispers of ancient lore, she journeyed through moonlit valleys and starlit meadows, embracing the journey that the night sky's canvas promised.

After days of travel, Leyla arrived at a mountaintop where an observatory stood—a place of reverence where seekers and dreamers gathered to contemplate the cosmos. In its heart stood the Celestial Weaver's Loom—a loom adorned with celestial symbols that seemed to shimmer with an ethereal light. Leyla approached the loom, and as she did, the stars above began to dance in intricate patterns.

With reverence, Leyla took hold of the Loom's threads and began to weave, allowing her fingers to be guided by the magic of the night sky. With each movement, the threads transformed, taking on shades of indigo, silver, and gold. She saw destinies unfolding—stories of heroes, lovers, and seekers who had left their mark on the tapestry of existence.

As constellations shifted and galaxies spun, Leyla's weaving took on a life of its own. The Celestial Weaver's Loom's magic seemed to amplify her understanding of destiny, and the threads wove tales that resonated with the heartbeat of humanity.

With each woven narrative, Leyla's understanding of the world expanded. She realised that the Celestial Weaver's Wisdom was not merely a set of symbols—it was a conduit through which the stories of destinies were told. She understood that the bond between artist and universe was a dance of interconnected energies—a symphony of creativity and guidance.

As the night deepened and stars filled the sky like diamonds, Leyla's weaving gradually came to an end, leaving her in the observatory's embrace bathed in a soft, otherworldly light. She knew that the Celestial Weaver's Loom had granted her a gift—the ability to shape not only artistic narratives but the destinies of humanity.

With gratitude in her heart, Leyla left the observatory and returned to her village, carrying with her the woven tapestries and the wisdom they contained.

She shared the tale of the "Celestial Weaver" and the insights she had gained with her fellow artists and dreamers, reminding them that the bond between weaver and universe was a dance of interconnected energies, and that the pursuit of shaping destinies and understanding was a symphony of creation and unity.

And so, dear listener, the story of Leyla and the "Celestial Weaver" teaches us that destiny is a journey that transcends the present moment, that the bond between artist and universe is a dance of interconnected energies, and that the essence of shaping narratives in the night sky is a timeless truth from the heart of ancient Persia.

The Enchanted Caravanserai

Unveiling Wonders in the Heart of a Mysterious Resting Place

In a realm where trade routes stretched like veins across the land and tales of the exotic lingered in the air, lived a young traveller named Farid. Farid's eyes held the wonder of a seeker, and his heart resonated with the mysteries of the unknown.

One evening, as Farid journeyed through the desert, he came upon a caravanserai unlike any other—an oasis of rest that seemed to shimmer with an otherworldly light. It was said that within the Enchanted Caravanserai, the power to unveil the wonders of distant lands and unlock the secrets of forgotten cultures was hidden.

Intrigued by the caravanserai's mysteries, Farid entered its gates. As he walked through its corridors, he felt the air hum with anticipation, and he saw merchants sharing tales of distant realms and traders showcasing treasures that spoke of ancient civilizations. Guided by the camaraderie of travellers and the whispers of the wind, he journeyed through the caravanserai's courtyards—courtyards adorned with mosaics, gardens scented with spices, and halls that held artefacts from lands both near and far.

With each step, Farid's understanding of the world expanded. He learned of silk roads that connected empires, tasted flavours that told stories of cultures, and saw artefacts that bore witness to the ebb and flow of human history. He realised that within the Enchanted Caravanserai, the boundaries between nations and eras were blurred—a testament to the interconnectedness of human experiences.

As the desert's heat gave way to the soothing cool of night and stars sprinkled the sky, Farid's exploration grew more profound. He encountered storytellers weaving narratives of dynasties and heroes, artisans crafting masterpieces that transcended time, and musicians playing melodies that echoed through ages.

With each wonder unveiled, Farid's heart swelled with a profound sense of unity. He knew that the Enchanted Caravanserai was not merely a resting place—it was a crossroads where the threads of cultures intertwined. He understood that the bond between traveller and tales was a dance of interconnected narratives—a symphony of exploration and exchange.

As the moon cast its gentle light over the caravanserai and the scent of spices lingered in the air, Farid's journey gradually came to an end, leaving him in the heart of the Enchanted Caravanserai bathed in a soft, otherworldly glow. He knew that the caravanserai had granted him a gift—the ability to experience not only his own travels but the collective journey of humanity.

With gratitude in his heart, Farid continued his journey and carried with him the insights and wonders he had gained. He shared the tale of the "Enchanted Caravanserai" and the wisdom of his experience with his fellow travellers and adventurers, reminding them that the bond between seeker and crossroads was a dance of interconnected narratives, and that the pursuit of exploration and understanding was a symphony of discovery and unity.

And so, dear listener, the story of Farid and the "Enchanted Caravanserai" teaches us that human experience is a journey that transcends borders, that the bond between traveller and tales is a dance of interconnected narratives, and that the essence of unveiling wonders in resting places is a timeless truth from the heart of ancient Persia.

The Whispering Sands

Listening to Echoes in the Heart of a Desert of Secrets

In a land where dunes stretched like waves frozen in time and the wind carried echoes of the past, lived a young nomad named Layla. Layla's eyes held the depth of a listener, and her heart resonated with the mysteries of the desert.

One morning, as Layla roamed the desert, she heard faint whispers in the wind—a chorus of voices that seemed to carry tales of forgotten ages. It was said that within the Whispering Sands, the power to connect with the echoes of history and unlock the stories of ancient civilizations was hidden.

Intrigued by the whispers, Layla ventured deeper into the desert. As she walked among the dunes, she felt the shifting sand beneath her feet and the caress of the breeze against her skin. Guided by the rhythm of the desert's heartbeat and the secrets whispered by the grains of sand, she journeyed through the desert's hidden pathways—oases that sparkled like jewels, valleys where rock formations painted pictures of time, and canyons that held the whispers of the ages.

With each step, Layla's understanding of the world expanded. She read the desert's glyphs, deciphered the stories told by ancient petroglyphs, and felt the echoes of travellers who had crossed these sands long before her. She realised that within the Whispering Sands, the boundaries between past and present were blurred—a testament to the timeless nature of the desert's tales.

As the sun painted the sky with hues of gold and amber, Layla's connection with the desert's echoes grew stronger. She heard tales of empires that had risen and fallen, saw images of caravans that had braved the desert's challenges, and understood the wisdom woven into the land's very fabric.

With each whispered narrative, Layla's heart swelled with a profound sense of reverence. She knew that the Whispering Sands were not merely a stretch of desert—they were a repository of hidden knowledge, a realm where seekers could listen to the stories that had shaped civilizations.

As twilight draped the desert in shades of purple and blue, Layla's journey gradually came to an end, leaving her on a sand dune bathed in a soft, otherworldly light. She knew that the Whispering Sands had granted her a gift—the ability to connect not only with the present but with the echoes of time itself.

With gratitude in her heart, Layla returned to her tribe, carrying with her the stories and wisdom she had encountered. She shared the tale of the "Whispering Sands" and the insights she had gained with her fellow nomads and seekers of knowledge, reminding them that the bond between listener and desert was a dance of interconnected echoes, and that the pursuit of understanding and connection was a symphony of humility and unity.

And so, dear listener, the story of Layla and the "Whispering Sands" teaches us that history is a journey that transcends the confines of time, that the bond between listener and desert is a dance of interconnected echoes, and that the essence of unveiling stories in the sand is a timeless truth from the heart of ancient Persia.

The Veiled Oracle

Unravelling Prophecies in the Heart of a Mystic Temple

In a city where domes and spires reached for the heavens and prophecies were whispered by the faithful, lived a young scholar named Zara. Zara's eyes held the curiosity of a seeker, and her heart resonated with the mysteries of destiny.

One day, as Zara studied ancient texts in a library, she received a vision—a vision of a mystical temple known as the Veiled Oracle. It was said that within the temple's hallowed halls, the power to unravel the threads of fate and uncover the truths of the unseen world was hidden.

Intrigued by the vision, Zara set out to find the Veiled Oracle. Guided by the stars and the whispers of mystics, she journeyed through bustling marketplaces and quiet alleys, embracing the journey that the temple's secrets promised.

After days of travel, Zara arrived at a hidden courtyard where the Veiled Oracle's temple stood—a sanctuary shrouded in mystery and veiled in mysticism. In its heart stood the Oracle's Veil—a tapestry adorned with intricate symbols that seemed to shimmer with an ethereal light. Zara stepped before the veil, and as she did, the air grew still, and the veil seemed to tremble with anticipation.

With reverence, Zara touched the Oracle's Veil, and as her fingers made contact, she felt a surge of energy course through her. Visions flooded her mind—prophecies of distant lands, tales of heroes' journeys, and the destinies of those who sought the temple's guidance.

As the tapestry's patterns shifted and the temple's candles flickered, Zara's understanding of the world expanded. She deciphered the symbols woven into the veil, interpreted the meanings hidden within its folds, and realised that the Oracle's Veil was not merely a piece of fabric—it was a conduit through which the truths of destiny were revealed.

With each prophecy unravelled, Zara's heart swelled with a profound sense of awe. She understood that the Veiled Oracle was not a fortune-teller—it was a beacon of insight that illuminated the interconnected nature of all existence. She knew that the bond between seeker and prophecy was a dance of interconnected energies—a symphony of guidance and self-discovery.

As the temple's lanterns cast a warm glow over the chamber and the scent of incense filled the air, Zara's experience gradually came to an end, leaving her before the Oracle's Veil bathed in a soft, otherworldly light.
She knew that the temple had granted her a gift—the ability to unravel not only the prophecies of the veil but the enigmas of destiny itself.

With gratitude in her heart, Zara left the temple and returned to her city, carrying with her the insights and revelations she had gained. She shared the tale of the "Veiled Oracle" and the wisdom of her experience with her fellow scholars and seekers of truth, reminding them that the bond between seeker and prophecy was a dance of interconnected energies, and that the pursuit of understanding and guidance was a symphony of humility and unity.

And so, dear listener, the story of Zara and the "Veiled Oracle" teaches us that destiny is a journey that transcends the confines of the visible world, that the bond between seeker and prophecy is a dance of interconnected energies, and that the essence of unravelling truths in mystical temples is a timeless truth from the heart of ancient Persia.

The Celestial Soothsayer

Reading the Future in the Patterns of the Night Sky

In a kingdom where palaces glistened with grandeur and the heavens were a tapestry of stars, lived a young soothsayer named Amir. Amir's eyes held the depth of a stargazer, and his heart resonated with the mysteries of the cosmos.

One night, as Amir observed the night sky, he received a vision—a vision of an ancient observatory known as the Celestial Nexus. It was said that within the observatory's chambers, the power to read the future in the patterns of the stars and planets was hidden, and those who possessed the celestial wisdom could foresee the destinies of individuals and kingdoms.

Intrigued by the vision, Amir embarked on a quest to find the Celestial Nexus. Guided by the constellations and the whispers of celestial spirits, he journeyed through lush gardens and towering palaces, embracing the journey that the observatory's insights promised.

After days of travel, Amir arrived at a hilltop where the Celestial Nexus stood—a sanctuary of knowledge and stargazing. In its centre stood the Nexus's Astrolabe—a complex instrument adorned with intricate markings that seemed to glow with an otherworldly light. Amir approached the astrolabe, and as he did, the stars above seemed to align in response to his presence.

With reverence, Amir touched the Astrolabe's surface and felt a surge of energy course through him. Visions flooded his mind—portents of events yet to unfold, omens woven into the movements of celestial bodies, and glimpses of fates entwined with the cosmos.

As the constellations danced and the night's embrace deepened, Amir's understanding of the world expanded. He read the stars like a book, interpreted the celestial symphony's melodies, and realised that the Astrolabe was not merely a tool—it was a key to unlocking the stories written in the skies.

With each prophecy unveiled, Amir's heart swelled with a profound sense of wonder. He knew that the Celestial Nexus was not a fortune-teller's den—it was a sanctum where the mysteries of the universe revealed themselves. He understood that the bond between soothsayer and cosmos was a dance of interconnected energies—a symphony of foresight and interpretation.

As the observatory's lanterns cast a soft glow over the chamber and the night's majesty unfolded above, Amir's celestial reading gradually came to an end, leaving him in the presence of the Astrolabe bathed in a soft, otherworldly light.
He knew that the observatory had granted him a gift—the ability to read not only the stars but the destinies that they held.

With gratitude in his heart, Amir left the observatory and returned to his kingdom, carrying with him the insights and revelations he had gained.

He shared the tale of the "Celestial Sooth sayer" and the wisdom of his celestial journey with his fellow soothsayers and seekers of foresight, reminding them that the bond between reader and cosmos was a dance of interconnected energies, and that the pursuit of foresight and understanding was a symphony of intuition and unity.

And so, dear listener, the story of Amir and the "Celestial Soothsayer" teaches us that destiny is a journey that transcends earthly boundaries, that the bond between reader and cosmos is a dance of interconnected energies, and that the essence of reading futures in the night sky is a timeless truth from the heart of ancient Persia.

The Sands of Unity

Discovering Bonds in the Heart of a Land of Legends

In a land where cities rose from the desert's embrace and tales of unity echoed through generations, lived a young historian named Mahin. Mahin's eyes held the wisdom of an observer, and her heart resonated with the power of shared stories.

One day, as Mahin explored ancient ruins, she stumbled upon a chamber unlike any other—a sanctuary of knowledge that seemed to carry echoes of ancient voices. It was said that within the Sands of Unity, the power to understand the connections between cultures and forge bonds of understanding was hidden.

Intrigued by the echoes, Mahin entered the chamber. As she walked among the artefacts, she felt the sands beneath her feet whisper secrets of unity, and she saw relics that bore the symbols of distant civilizations. Guided by the whispers of the past and the intertwined footprints of history, she journeyed through the chamber's displays—displays of artistry, texts of wisdom, and artefacts that spanned the ages.

With each step, Mahin's understanding of the world expanded. She read inscriptions that told of shared trade routes, deciphered languages that linked disparate lands, and saw artefacts that celebrated the common human experience. She realised that within the Sands of Unity, the boundaries between cultures and eras were blurred—a testament to the interconnectedness of humanity's journey.

As the sunlight filtered through the chamber's openings and cast intricate patterns on the sands, Mahin's exploration grew more profound. She encountered scrolls that carried stories of cooperation among kingdoms, sculptures that portrayed cultural exchange, and relics that spoke of alliances that transcended borders.

With each artefact discovered, Mahin's heart swelled with a profound sense of empathy. She knew that the Sands of Unity were not merely a collection of relics—they were a testament to the power of shared heritage. She understood that the bond between historian and history was a dance of interconnected narratives—a symphony of remembrance and connection.

As dusk's embrace painted the chamber in hues of warmth and shadow, Mahin's exploration gradually came to an end, leaving her surrounded by artefacts and echoes bathed in a soft, otherworldly light. She knew that the Sands of Unity had granted her a gift—the ability to understand not only the past but the threads that bound cultures together.

With gratitude in her heart, Mahin left the chamber and returned to her city, carrying with her the stories and insights she had encountered. She shared the tale of the "Sands of Unity" and the wisdom of her exploration with her fellow historians and seekers of shared understanding, reminding them that the bond between observer and history was a dance of interconnected narratives, and that the pursuit of unity and empathy was a symphony of remembrance and harmony.

And so, dear listener, the story of Mahin and the "Sands of Unity" teaches us that cultural connection is a journey that transcends geographical divides, that the bond between observer and history is a dance of interconnected narratives, and that the essence of discovering bonds in relics is a timeless truth from the heart of ancient Persia.

The Whispering Gardens

Listening to the Spirits in the Heart of a Serene Oasis

In a city where gardens bloomed with colours that rivalled the rainbow and stories of natural harmony filled the air, lived a young herbalist named Nasir. Nasir's eyes held the gentleness of a nurturer, and his heart resonated with the mysteries of the plant world.

One morning, as Nasir tended to his herbs, he heard faint whispers in the breeze—a chorus of voices that seemed to carry tales of the plants themselves. It was said that within the Whispering Gardens, the power to listen to the spirits of the plants and unlock the secrets of herbal remedies was hidden.

Intrigued by the whispers, Nasir entered the gardens. As he walked among the flowers, he felt the earth's pulse beneath his feet and the song of the birds that danced above. Guided by the rhythms of nature and the harmonies of the spirits, he journeyed through the garden's fragrant pathways—pathways adorned with blooms that held the wisdom of centuries, hidden clearings that resonated with the energy of the land, and groves that offered solace to seekers.

With each step, Nasir's understanding of the world expanded. He touched the petals of healing herbs, listened to the rustling leaves that whispered remedies, and felt the energies that flowed through the interconnected web of life. He realised that within the Whispering Gardens, the boundaries between healer and herb were blurred—a testament to the symbiotic dance between nature and humanity.

As the sun's rays filtered through the leaves and painted the garden in a palette of greens and golds, Nasir's connection with the garden's spirits grew stronger. He heard tales of ancient healers who had tended to these same plants, saw visions of rituals that honoured the natural world, and understood the wisdom woven into the very essence of the garden.

With each whispered insight, Nasir's heart swelled with a profound sense of reverence. He knew that the Whispering Gardens were not merely a collection of plants—they were a sanctuary where the spirits of nature revealed their secrets. He understood that the bond between herbalist and garden was a dance of interconnected energies—a symphony of healing and harmony.

As twilight's embrace painted the garden in shades of violet and azure, Nasir's experience gradually came to an end, leaving him in the heart of the Whispering Gardens bathed in a soft, otherworldly light.

He knew that the garden had granted him a gift—the ability to listen not only to the plants but to the spirits that nurtured them.

With gratitude in his heart, Nasir left the garden and returned to his village, carrying with him the insights and revelations he had gained.

He shared the tale of the "Whispering Gardens" and the wisdom of his connection with his fellow herbalists and seekers of natural balance, reminding them that the bond between healer and garden was a dance of interconnected energies, and that the pursuit of healing and harmony was a symphony of respect and unity.

And so, dear listener, the story of Nasir and the "Whispering Gardens" teaches us that natural harmony is a journey that transcends human borders, that the bond between healer and garden is a dance of interconnected energies, and that the essence of listening to the spirits in gardens is a timeless truth from the heart of ancient Persia.

The Lost Scroll of Wisdom

Seeking Knowledge in the Heart of a Forgotten Library

In a city where palaces of learning touched the sky and stories of forgotten wisdom echoed through the streets, lived a young scholar named Razi. Razi's eyes held the spark of discovery, and his heart resonated with the mysteries of ancient texts.

One day, as Razi perused manuscripts in a bustling library, he stumbled upon a chamber unlike any other—a chamber filled with dust-covered tomes and whispers of long-lost secrets. It was said that within the Lost Scroll of Wisdom, the power to uncover the insights of forgotten sages and unravel the truths of bygone eras was hidden.

Intrigued by the whispers, Razi ventured deeper into the chamber. As he touched the pages of ancient scrolls, he felt the weight of history in his hands and heard faint echoes of scholars who had once poured over these same words. Guided by the resonance of knowledge and the whispered thoughts of ages past, he journeyed through the chamber's rows of shelves—shelves adorned with texts that held the keys to understanding the world.

With each page turned, Razi's understanding of the world expanded. He deciphered scripts that held the knowledge of alchemists, interpreted the teachings of philosophers, and saw illustrations that told of scientific discoveries. He realised that within the Lost Scroll of Wisdom, the boundaries between eras and disciplines were blurred—a testament to the interconnected nature of human quest for understanding.

As daylight streamed through the chamber's windows and cast dancing patterns on the scrolls, Razi's exploration grew more profound. He encountered maps that charted unknown lands, diagrams that explained cosmic phenomena, and diagrams that spoke of the unity between the seen and unseen.

With each insight uncovered, Razi's heart swelled with a profound sense of reverence. He knew that the Lost Scroll of Wisdom was not merely a collection of texts—it was a sanctuary where the voices of forgotten thinkers were preserved. He understood that the bond between scholar and knowledge was a dance of interconnected narratives—a symphony of curiosity and respect.

As twilight's embrace painted the chamber in soft hues of orange and indigo, Razi's journey gradually came to an end, leaving him surrounded by ancient scrolls and echoes bathed in a soft, otherworldly light. He knew that the chamber had granted him a gift—the ability to uncover not only the texts but the insights and thoughts of those who had come before.

With gratitude in his heart, Razi left the chamber and returned to the world above, carrying with him the stories and insights he had encountered. He shared the tale of the "Lost Scroll of Wisdom" and the wisdom of his exploration with his fellow scholars and seekers of knowledge, reminding them that the bond between scholar and text was a dance of interconnected narratives, and that the pursuit of understanding and respect was a symphony of learning and unity.

And so, dear listener, the story of Razi and the "Lost Scroll of Wisdom" teaches us that knowledge is a journey that transcends the passage of time, that the bond between scholar and text is a dance of interconnected narratives, and that the essence of seeking wisdom in forgotten libraries is a timeless truth from the heart of ancient Persia.

The Celestial Symphony

Harmonising Lives in the Heart of a Musician's Haven

In a realm where melodies stirred the souls of its inhabitants and stories of harmonic unity resonated in the air, lived a young musician named Leyla. Leyla's eyes held the spark of creativity, and her heart resonated with the magic of music.

One evening, as Leyla played her instrument by a moonlit river, she received a vision—a vision of a legendary musician's enclave known as the Celestial Symphony. It was said that within the enclave's halls, the power to create harmonies that touched the essence of existence and bound souls together was hidden.

Intrigued by the vision, Leyla embarked on a journey to find the Celestial Symphony. Guided by the notes of the wind and the melodies of her heart, she journeyed through forests that whispered with secrets and valleys that hummed with unseen vibrations, embracing the path that the enclave's melodies promised.

After days of travel, Leyla arrived at a glen where the Celestial Symphony's halls stood—a haven of music and harmony. In its centre stood the Symphony's Conductor's Stand—a structure adorned with intricate carvings that seemed to resonate with an otherworldly energy. Leyla stepped before the stand, and as she did, the air seemed to come alive with the echoes of countless melodies.

With reverence, Leyla raised her instrument and began to play, allowing her heart to be guided by the magic of the enclave. With each note, the air seemed to shimmer, and Leyla's music intertwined with the symphony of the universe itself. She felt the presence of the spirits that had once graced the enclave's halls, heard echoes of melodies that spanned the ages, and understood that the Celestial Symphony was not merely a place—it was a conduit through which harmonies from beyond were brought to life.

With each chord struck, Leyla's understanding of the world expanded. She composed melodies that celebrated the essence of nature, harmonies that conveyed the emotions of humanity, and refrains that spoke of unity among souls.
She realised that within the Celestial Symphony, the boundaries between instruments and souls were blurred—a testament to the interconnected nature of musical expression.

As the moon rose higher in the sky and the stars joined the celestial symphony, Leyla's connection with the enclave's energies grew stronger. She played melodies that transcended language, compositions that celebrated life's tapestry, and harmonies that bound souls in an eternal embrace.

With each resonating chord, Leyla's heart swelled with a profound sense of unity. She knew that the Celestial Symphony was not merely a stage—it was a realm where the music of existence played on. She understood that the bond between musician and melody was a dance of interconnected energies—a symphony of expression and connection.

As the night's magic enveloped the enclave and Leyla's music filled the air, her performance gradually came to an end, leaving her before the Conductor's Stand bathed in a soft, otherworldly light. She knew that the enclave had granted her a gift—the ability to harmonise not only melodies but the very essence of existence.

With gratitude in her heart, Leyla left the enclave and returned to her city, carrying with her the melodies and insights she had gained. She shared the tale of the "Celestial Symphony" and the wisdom of her musical journey with her fellow musicians and seekers of harmony, reminding them that the bond between musician and melody was a dance of interconnected energies, and that the pursuit of creating and sharing harmonies was a symphony of creativity and unity.

And so, dear listener, the story of Leyla and the "Celestial Symphony" teaches us that music is a journey that transcends the boundaries of instruments, that the bond between musician and melody is a dance of interconnected energies, and that the essence of harmonising lives in musician's enclaves is a timeless truth from the heart of ancient Persia.

The Radiant Alchemist

Unveiling Transformation in the Heart of an Enigmatic Laboratory

In a kingdom where experiments with the elements were revered and stories of mystical transformations echoed through the alleys, lived a young alchemist named Farzan. Farzan's eyes held the fire of inquiry, and his heart resonated with the mysteries of transmutation.

One morning, as Farzan worked in his modest laboratory, he received a vision—a vision of a hidden chamber known as the Radiant Alchemist's Sanctum. It was said that within the sanctum's walls, the power to unveil the secrets of alchemical metamorphosis and reveal the truths of the universe's building blocks was hidden.

Intrigued by the vision, Farzan embarked on a quest to find the Radiant Alchemist's Sanctum. Guided by the gleam of the sun and the whispered secrets of the elements, he journeyed through bustling marketplaces and tranquil groves, embracing the path that the sanctum's transformations promised.

After days of travel, Farzan arrived at a cave entrance where the Radiant Alchemist's Sanctum lay—a domain of elements and alchemical wonders. In its centre stood the Sanctum's Crucible—an apparatus adorned with intricate engravings that seemed to shimmer with a mystical light. Farzan stepped before the crucible, and as he did, the air seemed to crackle with energy.

With reverence, Farzan began his alchemical work, blending elements and compounds in harmony with the vision that had guided him. With each reaction, the crucible's contents glowed with ethereal radiance, and Farzan's understanding of the world expanded. He saw reactions that turned base substances into precious materials, transformations that resonated with the dance of atoms, and changes that reflected the universal principles of balance.

As the crucible's glow intensified and the sanctum's echoes whispered in his ears, Farzan's exploration grew more profound. He saw glimpses of the sanctum's previous inhabitants—alchemists who had communed with the elements and witnessed the dance of transformation. He understood that the Radiant Alchemist's Sanctum was not merely a laboratory—it was a place where the mysteries of transmutation were laid bare.

With each alchemical discovery, Farzan's heart swelled with a profound sense of wonder. He knew that the Radiant Alchemist's Sanctum was not a realm of magic—it was a domain of science, where the threads of the universe's fabric were woven together. He realised that the bond between alchemist and elements was a dance of interconnected energies—a symphony of experimentation and understanding.

As the sanctum's light bathed the chamber in brilliance and the elements responded to Farzan's touch, his journey gradually came to an end, leaving him before the Crucible bathed in a soft, otherworldly light. He knew that the sanctum had granted him a gift—the ability to unveil not only the transformations of substances but the profound metamorphosis of knowledge itself.

With gratitude in his heart, Farzan left the sanctum and returned to his kingdom, carrying with him the insights and revelations he had gained. He shared the tale of the "Radiant Alchemist" and the wisdom of his alchemical journey with his fellow seekers of knowledge and explorers of transformation, reminding them that the bond between alchemist and elements was a dance of interconnected energies, and that the pursuit of experimentation and discovery was a symphony of curiosity and unity.

And so, dear listener, the story of Farzan and the "Radiant Alchemist" teaches us that transformation is a journey that transcends the boundaries of materials, that the bond between alchemist and elements is a dance of interconnected energies, and that the essence of unveiling secrets in enigmatic laboratories is a timeless truth from the heart of ancient Persia.

The Starlit Labyrinth

Navigating Destiny in the Heart of an Astral Maze

In a world where constellations told stories of heroes and the mysteries of the night sky captivated the imagination, lived a young stargazer named Soraya. Soraya's eyes held the wonder of a dreamer, and her heart resonated with the mysteries of the cosmos.

One night, as Soraya gazed at the stars, she received a vision—a vision of a celestial labyrinth known as the Starlit Labyrinth. It was said that within the labyrinth's paths, the power to navigate destiny's threads and uncover the truths of one's life journey was hidden.

Intrigued by the vision, Soraya embarked on a quest to find the Starlit Labyrinth. Guided by the gleam of the stars and the whispered melodies of the constellations, she journeyed through fields that sparkled with nocturnal dew and valleys that echoed with cosmic harmonies, embracing the path that the labyrinth's mysteries promised.

After days of travel, Soraya arrived at a clearing where the Starlit Labyrinth lay—a maze of sparkling pathways and astral patterns. In its heart stood the Labyrinth's Star Gate—an arch adorned with intricate constellations that seemed to shimmer with an ethereal light. Soraya stepped beneath the gate, and as she did, the night seemed to come alive with a celestial chorus.

With reverence, Soraya ventured into the labyrinth's maze, allowing the stars above to guide her steps.

With each turn, the pathways shifted, and Soraya's understanding of the world expanded. She deciphered constellations that told tales of love and sacrifice, patterns that revealed the ebb and flow of time, and arrangements that spoke of the interconnected nature of the universe.

As the moon cast a soft glow over the labyrinth and the stars painted the sky with a myriad of lights, Soraya's journey grew more profound. She saw visions of her past, glimpses of her present, and hints of her potential futures. She realised that the Starlit Labyrinth was not merely a maze—it was a mirror that reflected the kaleidoscope of destiny itself.

With each revelation unveiled, Soraya's heart swelled with a profound sense of awe. She knew that the Starlit Labyrinth was not a realm of

fortune-telling—it was a space where one's connection to the cosmos was unveiled.
She understood that the bond between stargazer and sky was a dance of interconnected energies—a symphony of observation and self-discovery.

As the constellations continued their celestial dance and the labyrinth's mysteries whispered in her ears, Soraya's journey gradually came to an end, leaving her before the Star Gate bathed in a soft, otherworldly light. She knew that the labyrinth had granted her a gift—the ability to navigate not only the paths of the maze but the intricate threads of her own destiny.

With gratitude in her heart, Soraya left the labyrinth and returned to her village, carrying with her the insights and revelations she had gained. She shared the tale of the "Starlit Labyrinth" and the wisdom of her cosmic journey with her fellow stargazers and seekers of self-discovery, reminding them that the bond between observer and cosmos was a dance of interconnected energies, and that the pursuit of navigating destiny's threads was a symphony of wonder and unity.

And so, dear listener, the story of Soraya and the "Starlit Labyrinth" teaches us that destiny is a journey that transcends the confines of the earthly realm, that the bond between observer and cosmos is a dance of interconnected energies, and that the essence of navigating one's life journey in celestial mazes is a timeless truth from the heart of ancient Persia.

The Enchanted Oasis

Harmony Between Worlds in the Heart of a Mystical Oasis

In a desert where tales of enchanted oases were whispered in hushed tones and stories of realms beyond the mortal gaze captured the imagination, lived a young traveller named Zahra. Zahra's eyes held the wonder of an explorer, and her heart resonated with the mysteries of hidden realms.

One day, as Zahra journeyed across the sands, she received a vision—a vision of a shimmering oasis known as the Enchanted Oasis. It was said that within the oasis's waters, the power to bridge the gap between the mortal realm and the mystical realms was hidden.

Intrigued by the vision, Zahra followed the oasis's trail, guided by the glimmer of its waters and the whispers of ethereal winds. She journeyed through dunes that shifted with secrets and canyons that echoed with hidden echoes, embracing the path that the oasis's mysteries promised.

After days of travel, Zahra arrived at a place where the Enchanted Oasis lay—a sanctuary of tranquillity and shimmering waters. In its centre stood the Oasis's Reflection Pool—a pool adorned with intricate patterns that seemed to reflect the very fabric of reality itself. Zahra approached the pool, and as she did, the air seemed to dance with an enchanting light.

With reverence, Zahra gazed into the pool's waters, allowing her thoughts to mingle with the ripples. With each reflection, the waters offered glimpses of otherworldly realms, whispered tales of beings that straddled the boundaries between worlds, and showcased the intricate interplay of different planes of existence. She realised that within the Enchanted Oasis, the boundaries between the known and unknown were blurred—a testament to the interconnected nature of reality.

As the sun dipped below the horizon and cast hues of gold and crimson across the sky, Zahra's connection with the oasis's energies deepened. She glimpsed visions of spirit beings who had graced the oasis's shores, heard echoes of their wisdom and insights, and understood that the Enchanted Oasis was not merely a place—it was a threshold that led to the realms of the mystical.

With each mystical insight, Zahra's heart swelled with a profound sense of reverence. She knew that the Enchanted Oasis was not an illusion—it was a gateway to the realms that lay beyond human perception. She understood that the bond between traveller and oasis was a dance of interconnected energies—a symphony of exploration and understanding.

As twilight's embrace painted the oasis in shades of amethyst and azure, Zahra's experience gradually came to an end, leaving her before the Reflection Pool bathed in a soft, otherworldly light. She knew that the oasis had granted her a gift—the ability to glimpse not only the oasis's waters but the interconnected tapestry of existence itself.

With gratitude in her heart, Zahra left the oasis and returned to her desert, carrying with her the insights and revelations she had gained. She shared the tale of the "Enchanted Oasis" and the wisdom of her mystical journey with her fellow travellers and seekers of hidden truths, reminding them that the bond between explorer and oasis was a dance of interconnected energies, and that the pursuit of bridging the gap between worlds was a symphony of wonder and unity.

And so, dear listener, the story of Zahra and the "Enchanted Oasis" teaches us that hidden realms are a journey that transcends the boundaries of perception, that the bond between traveller and oasis is a dance of interconnected energies, and that the essence of bridging the gap between worlds in mystical oases is a timeless truth from the heart of ancient Persia.

The Whispering Tapestries

Unravelling Secrets in the Heart of a Royal Palace

In a kingdom where history was woven into the very fabric of the land and stories of ancient rulers echoed through grand halls, lived a young historian named Zareen. Zareen's eyes held the curiosity of a seeker, and her heart resonated with the mysteries of royal heritage.

One day, as Zareen explored the corridors of a majestic palace, she stumbled upon a chamber unlike any other—a chamber adorned with intricate tapestries that seemed to hold hidden stories. It was said that within the Whispering Tapestries, the power to unravel the secrets of royal lineage and reveal the truths of bygone reigns was hidden.

Intrigued by the tales, Zareen stepped into the chamber. As she ran her fingers over the woven threads, she felt the vibrations of past voices and caught glimpses of historical scenes that had been immortalised in the tapestries. Guided by the whispers of time and the intricate patterns before her, she journeyed through the chamber's display—scenes of coronations, battles, alliances, and moments of profound significance.

With each tapestry examined, Zareen's understanding of the world expanded. She interpreted symbols that held the stories of dynasties, deciphered imagery that depicted the rise and fall of empires, and saw threads that told of the interconnected destinies of rulers and subjects. She realised that within the Whispering Tapestries, the boundaries between monarch and populace were blurred—a testament to the interwoven nature of a kingdom's legacy.

As the daylight filtered through the chamber's windows and illuminated the tapestries' colours, Zareen's exploration grew more profound. She encountered motifs that celebrated cultural exchange, depictions that spoke of diplomacy between kingdoms, and images that revealed the wisdom of rulers who had shaped history. She understood that the Whispering Tapestries were not merely works of art—they were portals through which the past whispered its stories.

With each narrative unveiled, Zareen's heart swelled with a profound sense of connection. She knew that the Whispering Tapestries were not just decorative adornments—they were vessels that held the echoes of ancient lives. She understood that the bond between historian and history was a dance of interconnected narratives—a symphony of preservation and understanding.

As dusk's embrace painted the chamber in hues of twilight and shadow, Zareen's journey gradually came to an end, leaving her surrounded by tapestries and echoes bathed in a soft, otherworldly light. She knew that the Whispering Tapestries had granted her a gift—the ability to unravel not only the threads of the tapestries but the intricate stories they contained.

With gratitude in her heart, Zareen left the chamber and returned to her study, carrying with her the stories and insights she had encountered. She shared the tale of the "Whispering Tapestries" and the wisdom of her exploration with her fellow historians and seekers of royal heritage, reminding them that the bond between historian and history was a dance of interconnected narratives, and that the pursuit of unravelling secrets and understanding the past was a symphony of remembrance and unity.

And so, dear listener, the story of Zareen and the "Whispering Tapestries" teaches us that royal lineage is a journey that transcends the passage of time, that the bond between historian and history is a dance of interconnected narratives, and that the essence of unravelling secrets in the fabric of royal palaces is a timeless truth from the heart of ancient Persia.

The Eternal Flame

Guardianship of Wisdom in the Heart of a Sacred Temple

In a land where sacred temples held the knowledge of ages and stories of devotion echoed through sacred chambers, lived a young priestess named Neda. Neda's eyes held the serenity of a guardian, and her heart resonated with the mysteries of divine wisdom.

One night, as Neda tended to the sacred flame in her temple, she received a vision—a vision of an eternal flame known as the Eternal Flame. It was said that within the flame's flickering light, the power to guard the truths of ancient knowledge and protect the sanctity of a nation's heritage was hidden.

Intrigued by the vision, Neda embarked on a pilgrimage to find the Eternal Flame. Guided by the luminance of its light and the whispers of the divine, she journeyed through sacred groves that hummed with spiritual energies and mountains that echoed with transcendent truths, embracing the path that the flame's illumination promised.

After days of devotion, Neda arrived at a sanctuary where the Eternal Flame blazed—a beacon of timeless wisdom and spiritual enlightenment. In its centre stood the Flame's Altar—and altar adorned with intricate symbols that seemed to radiate with an ethereal energy. Neda approached the altar, and as she did, the air seemed to resonate with a celestial harmony.

With reverence, Neda tended to the Eternal Flame, offering her prayers and absorbing its radiant light. With each flicker, the flame seemed to hold the essence of ages past, and Neda's understanding of the world expanded. She saw visions of ancient texts that had been illuminated by the flame's glow, felt the energy of scholars who had meditated in its presence, and understood that the Eternal Flame was not just a source of light—it was a custodian of the nation's collective wisdom.

As the stars glittered in the night sky and the Eternal Flame's glow painted the sanctuary in an ethereal radiance, Neda's connection with the flame's energies deepened. She felt the presence of seekers who had come before her, heard echoes of prayers that had been offered, and realised that the Eternal Flame was not merely a physical fire—it was a bridge between realms, a manifestation of the divine's guidance.

With each prayer uttered, Neda's heart swelled with a profound sense of devotion. She knew that the Eternal Flame was not a simple fire—it was a conduit through which wisdom flowed.
She understood that the bond between priestess and flame was a dance of interconnected energies—a symphony of reverence and enlightenment.

As the night's stillness embraced the sanctuary and the Eternal Flame's light danced in the air, Neda's experience gradually came to an end, leaving her before the Altar bathed in a soft, otherworldly light. She knew that the flame had granted her a gift—the ability to guard not only the flame's light but the divine wisdom it illuminated.

With gratitude in her heart, Neda left the sanctuary and returned to her temple, carrying with her the insights and revelations she had gained. She shared the tale of the "Eternal Flame" and the wisdom of her spiritual journey with her fellow priestesses and seekers of divine guidance, reminding them that the bond between guardian and flame was a dance of interconnected energies, and that the pursuit of guarding wisdom and kindling the flame of enlightenment was a symphony of devotion and unity.

And so, dear listener, the story of Neda and the "Eternal Flame" teaches us that divine wisdom is a journey that transcends human lifetimes, that the bond between guardian and flame is a dance of interconnected energies, and that the essence of tending to the flame of enlightenment in sacred temples is a timeless truth from the heart of ancient Persia.

The Oracle's Gaze

Guidance of Fate in the Heart of a Mysterious Cave

In a realm where oracles channelled the whispers of destiny and stories of foreseen futures echoed through shadowed caverns, lived a young seer named Darius. Darius's eyes held the depth of insight, and his heart resonated with the mysteries of fate.

One morning, as Darius explored the wild landscapes, he received a vision—a vision of a hidden cave known as the Oracle's Gaze. It was said that within the cave's depths, the power to glean insights into the threads of destiny and uncover the truths of intertwining fates was hidden.

Intrigued by the vision, Darius ventured into the wilderness, guided by the call of his seer's intuition and the whispers of the wind. He journeyed through meadows that rustled with ancient secrets and cliffs that whispered with glimpses of the unknown, embracing the path that the cave's revelations promised.

After days of travel, Darius arrived at a cavern where the Oracle's Gaze lay—a sanctuary of enigmatic wisdom and prophetic visions. In its heart stood the Gaze's Reflecting Pool—a pool adorned with intricate symbols that seemed to mirror the dance of the cosmos. Darius approached the pool, and as he did, the air seemed to pulse with a heightened energy.

With reverence, Darius gazed into the Reflecting Pool, allowing his consciousness to merge with its depths. With each ripple, the pool seemed to reflect not only his own presence, but the destinies of souls and the interplay of choices that shaped the world. He realised that within the Oracle's Gaze, the boundaries between the individual and the collective were blurred—a testament to the interconnected nature of fate.

As the sun cast dappled patterns on the water's surface and the pool's reflections whispered of hidden truths, Darius's exploration grew more profound. He caught glimpses of paths that diverged and converged, saw moments of decision that rippled across time, and witnessed the tapestry of lives that wove into a grand design. He understood that the Oracle's Gaze was not merely a reflective surface—it was a portal through which the future's potential unfolded.

With each vision unveiled, Darius's heart swelled with a profound sense of responsibility. He knew that the Oracle's Gaze was not a crystal ball—it was a doorway to understanding and insight. He realised that the bond between seer and oracle was a dance of interconnected energies—a symphony of perception and interpretation.
As twilight's hues embraced the cavern and the Reflecting Pool's whispers echoed in the air, Darius's experience gradually came to an end, leaving him before the Reflecting Pool bathed in a soft, otherworldly light. He knew that the Oracle's Gaze had granted him a gift—the ability to peer not only into the pool's waters but into the intricacies of the future itself.

With gratitude in his heart, Darius left the cavern and returned to his village, carrying with him the insights and revelations he had gained. He shared the tale of the "Oracle's Gaze" and the wisdom of his visionary journey with his fellow seers and seekers of destiny, reminding them that the bond between seer and oracle was a dance of interconnected energies, and that the pursuit of understanding fate's threads and uncovering hidden truths was a symphony of intuition and unity.

And so, dear listener, the story of Darius and the "Oracle's Gaze" teaches us that destiny's threads are a journey that transcends individual lives, that the bond between seer and oracle is a dance of interconnected energies, and that the essence of gazing into the future in mysterious caverns is a timeless truth from the heart of ancient Persia.

The Luminous Bazaar

Confluence of Cultures in the Heart of a Trade City

In a bustling city where markets teemed with treasures from across lands and stories of cultural exchange echoed through vibrant bazaars, lived a young merchant named Layla. Layla's eyes held the spark of curiosity, and her heart resonated with the beauty of diverse cultures.

One day, as Layla wandered through the maze of market stalls, she stumbled upon a plaza unlike any other—a plaza illuminated by lanterns and adorned with exotic goods. It was said that within the Luminous Bazaar, the power to weave connections between distant lands and foster understanding between peoples was hidden.

Intrigued by the stories, Layla ventured into the plaza. As she touched the textures of foreign fabrics and savoured the scents of spices from distant shores, she felt a harmony that transcended language and culture. Guided by the mingling aromas and the resonant laughter of visitors, she journeyed through the bazaar's corners—stalls offering fabrics, trinkets, and delicacies from every corner of the world.

With each interaction, Layla's understanding of the world expanded. She learned phrases from languages she had never heard, tasted dishes that carried the essence of far-off lands, and saw crafts that told stories of ancestral traditions. She realised that within the Luminous Bazaar, the boundaries between nations and peoples were blurred—a testament to the interwoven tapestry of humanity.

As the lanterns illuminated the bazaar's bustling activity and the mingling voices created a symphony of diversity, Layla's exploration grew more profound. She encountered merchants who shared stories of their homelands, artisans who showcased their craft's significance, and travellers who spoke of shared experiences across cultures. She understood that the Luminous Bazaar was not merely a marketplace—it was a space where the bridges between cultures were forged.

With each connection made, Layla's heart swelled with a profound sense of unity. She knew that the Luminous Bazaar was not just a collection of stalls—it was a haven where cultural melodies harmonised. She understood that the bond between merchant and marketplace was a dance of interconnected energies—a symphony of exchange and appreciation.

As the night's embrace painted the plaza in a myriad of colours and the sounds of diverse languages filled the air, Layla's experience gradually came to an end, leaving her amidst the lantern-lit bazaar bathed in a soft, otherworldly light. She knew that the plaza had granted her a gift—the ability to connect not only with goods but with the shared stories and aspirations of people from around the world.
With gratitude in her heart, Layla left the bazaar and returned to her trading post, carrying with her the connections and insights she had gained.

She shared the tale of the "Luminous Bazaar" and the wisdom of her cultural journey with her fellow merchants and seekers of cross-cultural understanding, reminding them that the bond between merchant and marketplace was a dance of interconnected energies, and that the pursuit of fostering connections and embracing diversity was a symphony of exchange and unity.

And so, dear listener, the story of Layla and the "Luminous Bazaar" teaches us that cultural exchange is a journey that transcends geographical borders, that the bond between merchant and marketplace is a dance of interconnected energies, and that the essence of fostering connections in vibrant bazaars is a timeless truth from the heart of ancient Persia.

The Resonant Oasis

Harmony in Diversity in the Heart of a Cultural Haven

In a land where diverse traditions coalesced and stories of unity through diversity echoed through cultural enclaves, lived a young musician named Amir. Amir's eyes held the warmth of acceptance, and his heart resonated with the power of harmonious collaboration.

One evening, as Amir wandered through the bustling heart of his city, he stumbled upon an oasis unlike any other—an oasis adorned with vibrant tapestries, painted murals, and diverse musical instruments. It was said that within the Resonant Oasis, the power to weave melodies that blended diverse musical traditions and fostered unity was hidden.

Intrigued by the tales, Amir stepped into the oasis. As he listened to the rhythms of drums from one corner and the melodies of strings from another, he felt a harmony that transcended musical genres and cultural backgrounds. Guided by the mingling sounds and the shared laughter of visitors, he journeyed through the oasis's spaces—rooms where musicians from every corner of the world practised their art.

With each performance witnessed, Amir's understanding of the world expanded. He heard scales that resonated with ancient traditions, melodies that carried the essence of distant lands, and harmonies that told stories of diverse origins. He realised that within the Resonant Oasis, the boundaries between musical styles and cultural heritages were blurred—a testament to the interwoven symphony of humanity.

As the music filled the air with its enchanting tapestry and the fusion of instruments created a harmonious mosaic, Amir's exploration grew more profound. He encountered artists who shared stories of their musical lineage, composers who embraced influences from across cultures, and listeners who reveled in the shared experiences across genres. He understood that the Resonant Oasis was not merely a performance space—it was a haven where musical bridges were constructed.

With each note that resonated, Amir's heart swelled with a profound sense of togetherness. He knew that the Resonant Oasis was not just an artistic venue—it was a sanctuary where diverse voices harmonised. He understood that the bond between musician and oasis was a dance of interconnected energies—a symphony of collaboration and appreciation.

As the night's embrace painted the oasis in warm hues and the melodies filled the air with their resonance, Amir's experience gradually came to an end, leaving him amidst the musical enclave bathed in a soft, otherworldly light.
He knew that the oasis had granted him a gift—the ability to blend not only musical notes but the diverse stories and emotions they carried.

With gratitude in his heart, Amir left the oasis and returned to his home, carrying with him the harmonies and insights he had gained.

He shared the tale of the "Resonant Oasis" and the wisdom of his musical journey with his fellow musicians and seekers of unity through diversity, reminding them that the bond between artist and sanctuary was a dance of interconnected energies, and that the pursuit of harmonising diversity and embracing collaboration was a symphony of artistry and unity.

And so, dear listener, the story of Amir and the "Resonant Oasis" teaches us that musical collaboration is a journey that transcends individual genres, that the bond between artist and sanctuary is a dance of interconnected energies, and that the essence of harmonising diversity in cultural havens is a timeless truth from the heart of ancient Persia.

The Mosaic of Friendship

Weaving Bonds in the Heart of a Multicultural Neighborhood

In a city where diverse communities thrived and stories of cross-cultural friendships echoed through vibrant neighbourhoods, lived a young artist named Samira. Samira's eyes held the warmth of empathy, and her heart resonated with the beauty of building connections.

One day, as Samira walked through the cobbled streets of her multicultural neighbourhood, she stumbled upon a courtyard unlike any other—a courtyard adorned with murals, sculptures, and vibrant gardens. It was said that within the Mosaic of Friendship, the power to create artworks that celebrated shared experiences and nurtured bonds between neighbours was hidden.

Intrigued by the tales, Samira stepped into the courtyard. As she studied the depictions of families, friends, and communities from diverse backgrounds, she felt an understanding that transcended language and ethnicity.
Guided by the colours of the murals and the laughter of children playing together, she journeyed through the courtyard's spaces—corners that held sculptures symbolising unity, and walls that displayed artworks reflecting the harmony between different cultures.

With each artwork observed, Samira's understanding of the world expanded. She saw images of celebrations that intertwined traditions, depictions of neighbours sharing meals, and representations of friendships that crossed cultural boundaries. She realised that within the Mosaic of Friendship, the lines between nationalities and backgrounds were blurred—a testament to the interconnected tapestry of human connections.

As the sunlight filtered through the leaves and illuminated the courtyard's vibrant displays, Samira's exploration grew more profound. She encountered storytellers who shared tales from different corners of the world, witnessed gatherings that celebrated cultural holidays, and engaged in conversations that celebrated the enriching diversity of their community. She understood that the Mosaic of Friendship was not just a courtyard—it was a gathering space where bonds were woven.

With each interaction, Samira's heart swelled with a profound sense of belonging. She knew that the Mosaic of Friendship was not just an artistic installation—it was a sanctuary where connections flourished.

She realised that the bond between artist and courtyard was a dance of interconnected energies—a symphony of creativity and togetherness.

As the day's warmth enveloped the courtyard and the mingling voices filled the air with their stories, Samira's experience gradually came to an end, leaving her amidst the vibrant enclave bathed in a soft, otherworldly light. She knew that the courtyard had granted her a gift—the ability to create not only artworks but the sense of community and unity they embodied.

With gratitude in her heart, Samira left the courtyard and returned to her studio, carrying with her the connections and insights she had gained. She shared the tale of the "Mosaic of Friendship" and the wisdom of her artistic journey with her fellow creators and seekers of cross-cultural understanding, reminding them that the bond between artist and courtyard was a dance of interconnected energies, and that the pursuit of weaving bonds and nurturing connections was a symphony of creativity and unity.

And so, dear listener, the story of Samira and the "Mosaic of Friendship" teaches us that cross-cultural friendships are a journey that transcends geographical distances, that the bond between artist and courtyard is a dance of interconnected energies, and that the essence of nurturing bonds in vibrant neighbourhoods is a timeless truth from the heart of ancient Persia.

The Timekeeper's Hourglass

Unveiling Temporal Truths in the Heart of an Ancient Observatory

In a realm where celestial wonders danced across the night sky and stories of time's mysteries echoed through ancient observatories, lived a young astronomer named Arman. Arman's eyes held the wonder of an explorer, and his heart resonated with the mysteries of the cosmos.

One night, as Arman studied the stars from his observatory, he received a vision—a vision of a hidden chamber known as the Timekeeper's Hourglass. It was said that within the chamber's depths, the power to uncover the secrets of time's passage and glimpse the threads that wove the tapestry of history was hidden.

Intrigued by the vision, Arman embarked on a journey to find the Timekeeper's Hourglass. Guided by the constellations' guidance and the whispers of the universe, he journeyed through ancient ruins that held fragments of forgotten stories and mountains that echoed with the wisdom of ages, embracing the path that time's enigma promised.

After days of travel, Arman arrived at a chamber where the Timekeeper's Hourglass lay—a sanctuary of temporal wisdom and cosmic insights. In its centre stood the Hourglass's Pedestal—an altar adorned with intricate symbols that seemed to echo the rhythms of time itself. Arman approached the pedestal, and as he did, the air seemed to pulse with a timeless energy.

With reverence, Arman turned the hourglass, allowing the grains of sand to flow and mark the passage of moments. With each grain's descent, he felt the ebb and flow of history, and his understanding of the world expanded. He glimpsed scenes of civilizations rising and falling, witnessed the impact of pivotal events, and realised that within the Timekeeper's Hourglass, the boundaries between past, present, and future were blurred—a testament to the interwoven nature of time.

As the stars continued their silent journey across the firmament and the hourglass's sands whispered their stories, Arman's exploration grew more profound. He encountered visions of great scholars who had contemplated the mysteries of time, heard echoes of prophecies that had echoed through generations, and understood that the Timekeeper's Hourglass was not merely an instrument—it was a portal through which history's layers were unveiled.

With each insight revealed, Arman's heart swelled with a profound sense of reverence. He knew that the Timekeeper's Hourglass was not a simple timekeeping device—it was a doorway to the past's enigma. He understood that the bond between astronomer and hourglass was a dance of interconnected energies—a symphony of exploration and revelation.

As the night's canvas painted the chamber in deep hues and the hourglass's sands continued their journey, Arman's experience gradually came to an end, leaving him before the Pedestal bathed in a soft, otherworldly light.
He knew that the hourglass had granted him a gift—the ability to turn not only the hourglass's frame but the pages of history itself.

With gratitude in his heart, Arman left the chamber and returned to his observatory, carrying with him the insights and revelations he had gained. He shared the tale of the "Timekeeper's Hourglass" and the wisdom of his cosmic journey with his fellow astronomers and seekers of temporal truths, reminding them that the bond between explorer and hourglass was a dance of interconnected energies, and that the pursuit of unveiling history's layers and glimpsing the mysteries of time was a symphony of wonder and unity.

And so, dear listener, the story of Arman and the "Timekeeper's Hourglass" teaches us that history's tapestry is a journey that transcends the linear passage of moments, that the bond between explorer and hourglass is a dance of interconnected energies, and that the essence of unveiling temporal truths in ancient observatories is a timeless truth from the heart of ancient Persia.

The Celestial Weavers

Harmony Among Stars in the Heart of a Cosmic Haven

In a land where constellations painted stories across the night sky and tales of celestial harmony echoed through sacred sanctuaries, lived a young artist named Laila. Laila's eyes held the spark of creativity, and her heart resonated with the beauty of cosmic connections.

One evening, as Laila gazed at the stars from her rooftop, she received a vision—a vision of a hidden sanctuary known as the Celestial Weavers. It was said that within the sanctuary's walls, the power to create artworks that mirrored the dance of the stars and celebrated the bonds between celestial bodies was hidden.

Intrigued by the vision, Laila embarked on a quest to find the Celestial Weavers. Guided by the luminance of the constellations and the whispers of the cosmos, she journeyed through forests that whispered with cosmic secrets and rivers that mirrored the skies, embracing the path that the stars' harmony promised.

After days of travel, Laila arrived at a sanctuary where the Celestial Weavers worked—a haven of cosmic inspiration and artistic creation. In its centre stood the Weaver's Loom—an apparatus adorned with intricate patterns that seemed to capture the essence of the stars' dance. Laila approached the loom, and as she did, the air seemed to resonate with a celestial vibration.

With reverence, Laila wove her threads into the loom, creating patterns that mirrored the constellations above. With each movement, she felt the rhythm of the cosmos, and her understanding of the world expanded. She wove scenes of stars forming constellations, depicted the interconnected paths of planets, and realised that within the Celestial Weavers, the boundaries between the earthly and the cosmic were blurred—a testament to the interwoven symphony of the universe.

As the night's canvas illuminated the sanctuary and the loom's threads formed intricate tapestries, Laila's artistic journey grew more profound. She encountered master weavers who shared stories of celestial myths, saw depictions of cosmic events that had shaped history, and engaged in conversations that celebrated the beauty of the cosmos as a source of inspiration. She understood that the Celestial Weavers were not just artists—they were conduits through which the stars' tales were translated into art.

With each thread woven, Laila's heart swelled with a profound sense of connection. She knew that the Celestial Weavers were not just creators—they were cosmic interpreters.
She realised that the bond between artist and loom was a dance of interconnected energies—a symphony of creativity and cosmic alignment.

As the night's embrace deepened and the woven tapestries glowed with ethereal hues, Laila's experience gradually came to an end, leaving her before the Weaver's Loom bathed in a soft, otherworldly light. She knew that the loom had granted her a gift—the ability to weave not only threads but the harmonies of the stars themselves.

With gratitude in her heart, Laila left the sanctuary and returned to her abode, carrying with her the connections and insights she had gained. She shared the tale of the "Celestial Weavers" and the wisdom of her artistic journey with her fellow creators and seekers of cosmic inspiration, reminding them that the bond between artist and loom was a dance of interconnected energies, and that the pursuit of translating the dance of the stars into art and celebrating the beauty of the cosmos was a symphony of creativity and unity.

And so, dear listener, the story of Laila and the "Celestial Weavers" teaches us that cosmic harmony is a journey that transcends earthly boundaries, that the bond between artist and loom is a dance of interconnected energies, and that the essence of weaving cosmic connections in celestial havens is a timeless truth from the heart of ancient Persia.

The Essence of Memory

Retrieving Forgotten Histories in the Heart of an Ancient Library

In a realm where scrolls held the echoes of generations and stories of lost knowledge echoed through ancient libraries, lived a young scholar named Farid. Farid's eyes held the light of discovery, and his heart resonated with the mysteries of forgotten truths.

One day, as Farid explored the corridors of a sprawling library, he received a vision—a vision of a hidden chamber known as the Essence of Memory. It was said that within the chamber's depths, the power to retrieve histories that had faded from common knowledge and unveil the wisdom of antiquity was hidden.

Intrigued by the vision, Farid embarked on a quest to find the Essence of Memory. Guided by the ancient tomes' whispers and the scent of parchment that lingered in the air, he journeyed through dusty passages that held the keys to forgotten doors and chambers that resonated with the knowledge of ages, embracing the path that history's enigma promised.

After days of exploration, Farid arrived at a chamber where the Essence of Memory lay—a repository of lost knowledge and hidden truths. In its centre stood the Memory's Reflecting Pool—a pool adorned with intricate symbols that seemed to shimmer with the reflections of bygone eras. Farid approached the pool, and as he did, the air seemed to vibrate with the resonance of forgotten voices.

With reverence, Farid touched the water's surface, allowing its ripples to mirror the past's whispers. With each ripple, he felt the reverberations of history, and his understanding of the world expanded. He glimpsed records of civilizations that had vanished, read the wisdom of scholars whose works had been lost, and realised that within the Essence of Memory, the boundaries between eras were blurred—a testament to the interwoven tapestry of human progress.

As the candles illuminated the chamber's corners and the pool's reflections shimmered with hidden narratives, Farid's exploration grew more profound. He encountered texts that spoke of societies that had flourished and declined, deciphered symbols that held the keys to ancient languages, and engaged in conversations that celebrated the enduring power of knowledge. He understood that the Essence of

Memory was not merely a collection of forgotten lore—it was a sanctuary where the threads of history were rewoven.

With each insight gained, Farid's heart swelled with a profound sense of reverence. He knew that the Essence of Memory was not just a reservoir of forgotten truths—it was a conduit through which lost histories could be retrieved. He understood that the bond between scholar and reflecting pool was a dance of interconnected energies—a symphony of inquiry and revelation.

As the chamber's silence deepened and the water's reflections captured the essence of times long past, Farid's experience gradually came to an end, leaving him before the Reflecting Pool bathed in a soft, otherworldly light. He knew that the pool had granted him a gift—the ability to touch not only the water's surface but the echoes of history itself.

With gratitude in his heart, Farid left the chamber and returned to his study, carrying with him the insights and revelations he had gained. He shared the tale of the "Essence of Memory" and the wisdom of his historical journey with his fellow scholars and seekers of forgotten truths, reminding them that the bond between scholar and reflecting pool was a dance of interconnected energies, and that the pursuit of retrieving lost histories and unveiling the wisdom of antiquity was a symphony of exploration and unity.

And so, dear listener, the story of Farid and the "Essence of Memory" teaches us that history's echoes are a journey that transcends the passage of time, that the bond between scholar and reflecting pool is a dance of interconnected energies, and that the essence of retrieving forgotten truths in ancient libraries is a timeless truth from the heart of ancient Persia.

The Garden of Eternity

Harmony of Life and Death in the Heart of a Sacred Grove

In a land where nature's cycles mirrored stories of existence and stories of the connection between life and death echoed through ancient groves, lived a young healer named Azar. Azar's eyes held the depth of empathy, and her heart resonated with the mysteries of existence's tapestry.

One day, as Azar wandered through a verdant grove, she received a vision—a vision of a hidden garden known as the Garden of Eternity. It was said that within the garden's heart, the power to understand the delicate balance between life and death and embrace the essence of existence was hidden.

Intrigued by the vision, Azar ventured deeper into the grove. Guided by the rustling leaves and the songs of birds that echoed through the branches, she journeyed through paths that intertwined with the natural world and glades that seemed to hold the whisper of timeless truths, embracing the path that life's enigma promised.

After hours of exploration, Azar arrived at a clearing where the Garden of Eternity bloomed—a sanctuary of natural wisdom and the interconnectedness of all things. In its centre stood the Garden's Heart Tree—a tree adorned with intricate patterns that seemed to reflect the ebb and flow of existence. Azar approached the tree, and as she did, the air seemed to vibrate with the rhythm of life itself.

With reverence, Azar touched the bark of the Heart Tree, feeling its pulse beneath her fingertips. With each touch, she felt the resonance of life's cycles, and her understanding of the world expanded. She witnessed flowers that blossomed and withered, watched animals that were born and returned to the earth, and realised that within the Garden of Eternity, the boundaries between growth and decay were blurred—a testament to the interwoven dance of nature.

As the sun filtered through the leaves and the wind carried the fragrances of blossoms, Azar's exploration grew more profound. She encountered healers who shared tales of herbal remedies that harmonised with nature's rhythms, observed rituals that celebrated the passage of seasons, and engaged in conversations that celebrated the interconnectedness of all living things. She understood that the Garden of Eternity was not just a collection of flora—it was a space where life's unity was honoured.

With each moment observed, Azar's heart swelled with a profound sense of reverence. She knew that the Garden of Eternity was not just a grove—it was a haven where the cycles of existence were celebrated. She realised that the bond between healer and heart tree was a dance of interconnected energies—a symphony of healing and harmony.

As the grove's serenity deepened and the Heart Tree's branches embraced the sky, Azar's experience gradually came to an end, leaving her before the Heart Tree bathed in a soft, otherworldly light. She knew that the tree had granted her a gift—the ability to touch not only its bark but the pulse of life that flowed through all beings.

With gratitude in her heart, Azar left the grove and returned to her healing sanctuary, carrying with her the connections and insights she had gained. She shared the tale of the "Garden of Eternity" and the wisdom of her natural journey with her fellow healers and seekers of life's mysteries, reminding them that the bond between healer and heart tree was a dance of interconnected energies, and that the pursuit of embracing the cycles of existence and celebrating the unity of all life was a symphony of healing and unity.

And so, dear listener, the story of Azar and the "Garden of Eternity" teaches us that life's rhythms are a journey that transcends individual existence, that the bond between healer and heart tree is a dance of interconnected energies, and that the essence of embracing the interconnectedness of all life in ancient groves is a timeless truth from the heart of ancient Persia.

The Whispers of the Sands

Echoes of Ancient Wisdom in the Heart of a Desert Oasis

In a realm where shifting sands told tales of ages past and stories of ancestral wisdom echoed through desert oases, lived a young nomad named Zahra. Zahra's eyes held the sparkle of curiosity, and her heart resonated with the secrets of ancient knowledge.

One day, as Zahra wandered through the dunes and palm-fringed oases, she received a vision—a vision of a hidden wellspring known as the Whispers of the Sands. It was said that within the wellspring's depths, the power to hear the echoes of long-forgotten teachings and connect with the wisdom of desert travellers was hidden.

Intrigued by the vision, Zahra embarked on a journey to find the Whispers of the Sands. Guided by the desert winds and the footprints left by those who had journeyed before, she navigated through dunes that held the footprints of generations and caverns that seemed to resonate with the essence of the land itself, embracing the path that the desert's enigma promised.

After days of traversing the arid landscapes, Zahra arrived at an oasis where the Whispers of the Sands were said to flow—a sanctuary of ancestral knowledge and the shared experiences of travellers. In its centre stood the Wellspring's Basin—a basin adorned with intricate motifs that seemed to mirror the patterns of wind-sculpted sand. Zahra approached the basin, and as she did, the air seemed to carry the echoes of ages.

With reverence, Zahra cupped her hands to the water's surface, feeling its touch against her skin. With each touch, she felt the vibrations of ancient teachings, and her understanding of the world expanded. She heard echoes of tales told around desert campfires, listened to stories of journeys through unforgiving landscapes, and realised that within the Whispers of the Sands, the boundaries between the past and the present were blurred—a testament to the interwoven lore of desert lore.

As the sun cast its golden hue across the oasis and the breeze rustled the palm fronds, Zahra's exploration grew more profound. She encountered elders who shared tales of their travels across the desert expanse, saw patterns in the sand that hinted at hidden pathways, and engaged in conversations that celebrated the symbiotic relationship between travellers and the land. She understood that the Whispers of the Sands were not just tales—they were a treasure trove of wisdom from those who had journeyed through time and space.

With each echo heard, Zahra's heart swelled with a profound sense of respect. She knew that the Whispers of the Sands were not just stories—they were the voices of the desert itself. She realised that the bond between nomad and wellspring was a dance of interconnected energies—a symphony of discovery and connection.

As the oasis's tranquillity deepened and the wellspring's waters reflected the sky's hues, Zahra's experience gradually came to an end, leaving her before the Basin bathed in a soft, otherworldly light. She knew that the wellspring had granted her a gift—the ability to touch not only the water's surface but the echoes of desert wisdom.
With gratitude in her heart, Zahra left the oasis and returned to her nomadic tribe, carrying with her the connections and insights she had gained. She shared the tale of the "Whispers of the Sands" and the wisdom of her desert journey with her fellow nomads and seekers of ancestral knowledge, reminding them that the bond between traveller and wellspring was a dance of interconnected energies, and that the pursuit of hearing echoes of forgotten teachings and connecting with the wisdom of desert travellers was a symphony of exploration and unity.

And so, dear listener, the story of Zahra and the "Whispers of the Sands" teaches us that ancient wisdom is a journey that transcends temporal boundaries, that the bond between traveller and wellspring is a dance of interconnected energies, and that the essence of connecting with the wisdom of desert travellers in desert oases is a timeless truth from the heart of ancient Persia.

The Enchanted Minstrel

Melodies of Transformation in the Heart of a Mystic Forest

In a realm where nature and magic intertwined, and stories of musical enchantment echoed through mystical forests, lived a young minstrel named Roshan. Roshan's eyes held the sparkle of wonder, and his heart resonated with the power of harmonious melodies.

One twilight, as Roshan wandered through an ancient forest, he received a vision—a vision of a hidden glade known as the Enchanted Harmony. It was said that within the glade's heart, the power to create melodies that resonated with the spirits of nature and transformed the world around was hidden.

Intrigued by the vision, Roshan ventured deeper into the forest. Guided by the rustling leaves and the whispering winds, he journeyed through groves where the trees seemed to dance to their own rhythm and clearings that held an aura of mystical energy, embracing the path that the forest's enigma promised.

After days of exploration, Roshan arrived at a glade where the Enchanted Harmony was said to bloom—a sanctuary of musical enchantment and the connection between minstrel and nature. In its centre stood the Harmony's Altar—an altar adorned with intricate carvings that seemed to mirror the patterns of nature's growth. Roshan approached the altar, and as he did, the air seemed to vibrate with a magical resonance.

With reverence, Roshan plucked his strings and began to play, allowing the melodies to weave through the forest air. With each note, he felt the presence of ancient spirits, and his understanding of the world expanded. He heard echoes of birds joining in harmony, witnessed plants swaying to the rhythm, and realised that within the Enchanted Harmony, the boundaries between musician and nature were blurred—a testament to the interwoven symphony of existence.

As the moonlight filtered through the branches and the melodies swirled with ethereal enchantment, Roshan's musical journey grew more profound. He encountered creatures that emerged from the shadows to dance to his music, saw the leaves glow with magical hues, and engaged in conversations that celebrated the innate bond between music and nature. He understood that the Enchanted Harmony was not just an altar—it was a portal where melodies transformed the world around.

With each composition played, Roshan's heart swelled with a profound sense of awe. He knew that the Enchanted Harmony was not just a glade—it was a space where the realm of magic and music converged. He realised that the bond between minstrel and altar was a dance of interconnected energies—a symphony of creativity and transformation.

As the glade's aura deepened and the melodies continued their enchanting dance, Roshan's experience gradually came to an end, leaving him before the Altar bathed in a soft, otherworldly light. He knew that the altar had granted him a gift—the ability to strum not only his strings but the very threads of magic itself.

With gratitude in his heart, Roshan left the glade and returned to his musical journey, carrying with him the enchantment and insights he had gained. He shared the tale of the "Enchanted Harmony" and the wisdom of his mystical journey with his fellow minstrels and seekers of musical enchantment, reminding them that the bond between musician and altar was a dance of interconnected energies, and that the pursuit of creating melodies that resonated with the spirits of nature and transformed the world was a symphony of magic and unity.

And so, dear listener, the story of Roshan and the "Enchanted Harmony" teaches us that music's power is a journey that transcends earthly realms, that the bond between musician and altar is a dance of interconnected energies, and that the essence of creating melodies that enchant nature and transform the world is a timeless truth from the heart of ancient Persia.

The Labyrinth of Reflections

Journey of Self-Discovery in the Heart of an Ancient Palace

In a land where mirrors revealed deeper truths and stories of introspection echoed through opulent palaces, lived a young seeker named Layla. Layla's eyes held the spark of curiosity, and her heart resonated with the mysteries of self-discovery.

One day, as Layla roamed through the corridors of an ancient palace, she received a vision—a vision of a hidden chamber known as the Labyrinth of Reflections. It was said that within the chamber's depths, the power to confront one's inner self and unveil the layers of the soul was hidden.

Intrigued by the vision, Layla embarked on a quest to find the Labyrinth of Reflections. Guided by the glimmering lights of mirrors and the echoes of her footsteps in the hallways, she journeyed through opulent chambers that whispered of bygone eras and corridors that seemed to mirror her own path, embracing the journey that self-discovery's enigma promised.

After hours of wandering, Layla arrived at a chamber where the Labyrinth of Reflections was said to reside—a sanctuary of self-contemplation and the connection between seeker and soul. In its centre stood the Labyrinth's Mirror—a mirror adorned with intricate patterns that seemed to reflect the complexity of one's thoughts. Layla approached the mirror, and as she did, the air seemed to shimmer with a magical aura.

With reverence, Layla gazed into the mirror's surface, meeting her own reflection's gaze. With each moment of introspection, she felt the layers of her identity peeling away, and her understanding of the self expanded. She saw echoes of memories that had shaped her, confronted the shadows of doubts that lingered, and realised that within the Labyrinth of Reflections, the boundaries between exterior and interior were blurred—a testament to the interwoven nature of the human experience.

As the candlelight cast a soft glow across the chamber and the mirror's surface seemed to ripple with hidden meanings, Layla's introspective journey grew more profound. She encountered versions of herself that whispered of dreams and aspirations, saw glimpses of her past experiences that held keys to her present, and engaged in conversations that celebrated the interconnectedness of all aspects of the self. She understood that the Labyrinth of Reflections was not just a mirror—it was a portal through which the layers of the soul were unveiled.

With each reflection confronted, Layla's heart swelled with a profound sense of self-acceptance.
She knew that the Labyrinth of Reflections was not just a chamber—it was a space where one could embrace the entirety of their being. She realised that the bond between seeker and mirror was a dance of interconnected energies—a symphony of exploration and revelation.

As the chamber's ambiance deepened and the mirror's surface seemed to hold the essence of all that was, Layla's experience gradually came to an end, leaving her before the Mirror bathed in a soft, otherworldly light. She knew that the mirror had granted her a gift—the ability to gaze not only into her reflection but into the depths of her soul.

With gratitude in her heart, Layla left the chamber and returned to her personal journey, carrying with her the insights and revelations she had gained. She shared the tale of the "Labyrinth of Reflections" and the wisdom of her introspective journey with her fellow seekers and explorers of self-discovery, reminding them that the bond between seeker and mirror was a dance of interconnected energies, and that the pursuit of confronting one's inner self and unveiling the layers of the soul was a symphony of introspection and unity.

And so, dear listener, the story of Layla and the "Labyrinth of Reflections" teaches us that self-discovery is a journey that transcends the surface of appearance, that the bond between seeker and mirror is a dance of interconnected energies, and that the essence of confronting one's inner self in ancient palaces is a timeless truth from the heart of ancient Persia.

The Chalice of Dreams

Unveiling Prophecies in the Heart of a Mystic Temple

In a realm where visions of the future intermingled with the present, and stories of prophetic insight echoed through mystical temples, lived a young oracle named Cyrus. Cyrus's eyes held the depth of clairvoyance, and his heart resonated with the secrets of fate.

One night, as Cyrus meditated within the walls of an ancient temple, he received a vision—a vision of a hidden chamber known as the Chalice of Dreams. It was said that within the chamber's depths, the power to glimpse prophecies and interpret the symbols of destiny was hidden.

Intrigued by the vision, Cyrus embarked on a quest to find the Chalice of Dreams. Guided by the flickering flames of ancient torches and the whispers of the temple's ethereal energies, he journeyed through halls that resonated with the echoes of foretelling and chambers that seemed to pulse with the rhythm of time, embracing the path that fate's enigma promised.

After days of meditative wandering, Cyrus arrived at a chamber where the Chalice of Dreams was said to rest—a sanctuary of prophetic insight and the connection between oracle and destiny. In its centre stood the Chalice's Altar—an altar adorned with intricate symbols that seemed to reflect the cosmos itself. Cyrus approached the altar, and as he did, the air seemed to vibrate with a mystic resonance.

With reverence, Cyrus held the chalice and closed his eyes, allowing the currents of his thoughts to flow. With each moment of deep focus, he felt the threads of fate unravel, and his understanding of the world expanded. He glimpsed scenes of events yet to pass, interpreted symbols that held the keys to unfolding destinies, and realised that within the Chalice of Dreams, the boundaries between the present and the future were blurred—a testament to the interwoven tapestry of time.

As the temple's incense wafted through the air and the chalice's contents shimmered with prophetic revelations, Cyrus's journey of foresight grew more profound. He encountered seers who had come before him, saw visions of pivotal moments that shaped civilizations, and engaged in conversations that celebrated the interconnected nature of all occurrences. He understood that the Chalice of Dreams was not just a vessel—it was a vessel through which prophecies were received.

With each revelation glimpsed, Cyrus's heart swelled with a profound sense of responsibility. He knew that the Chalice of Dreams was not just an object—it was a conduit through which he could interpret the threads of destiny. He realised that the bond between oracle and altar was a dance of interconnected energies—a symphony of foresight and interpretation.

As the chamber's atmosphere deepened and the chalice's contents continued to shimmer with cryptic messages, Cyrus's experience gradually came to an end, leaving him before the Altar bathed in a soft, otherworldly light. He knew that the altar had granted him a gift—the ability to hold not only the chalice but the symbols of fate itself.

With gratitude in his heart, Cyrus left the chamber and returned to his role as an oracle, carrying with him the insights and revelations he had gained. He shared the tale of the "Chalice of Dreams" and the wisdom of his prophetic journey with his fellow seers and seekers of fate's mysteries, reminding them that the bond between oracle and altar was a dance of interconnected energies, and that the pursuit of glimpsing prophecies and interpreting the symbols of destiny was a symphony of foresight and unity.

And so, dear listener, the story of Cyrus and the "Chalice of Dreams" teaches us that destiny's tapestry is a journey that transcends the boundaries of time, that the bond between oracle and altar is a dance of interconnected energies, and that the essence of glimpsing prophecies and interpreting the symbols of fate in ancient temples is a timeless truth from the heart of ancient Persia.

The Sands of Serenity

Harmony of Body and Mind in the Heart of a Desert Retreat

In a land where tranquillity merged with the vast desert landscapes, and stories of holistic well-being echoed through serene retreats, lived a young healer named Darius. Darius's eyes held the gaze of calm, and his heart resonated with the art of balance.

One day, as Darius walked across the desert sands, he received a vision—a vision of a hidden oasis known as the Sands of Serenity. It was said that within the oasis's heart, the power to restore the equilibrium between body and mind and embrace the essence of well-being was hidden.

Intrigued by the vision, Darius set out to find the Sands of Serenity. Guided by the warm caress of the desert breeze and the distant rustle of palm fronds, he journeyed through shifting dunes that seemed to mirror the fluctuations of life and valleys that held a sense of inner peace, embracing the path that the desert's enigma promised.

After days of traversing the arid landscapes, Darius arrived at an oasis where the Sands of Serenity were said to grace—a sanctuary of holistic rejuvenation and the connection between healer and nature. In its centre stood the Oasis's Pond—an expanse adorned with tranquil patterns that seemed to reflect the serenity of the desert's heart. Darius approached the pond, and as he did, the air seemed to carry the echoes of inner calm.

With reverence, Darius dipped his hands into the pond's waters, feeling their soothing touch against his skin. With each moment of immersion, he felt the harmony of body and mind being restored, and his understanding of the world expanded. He experienced echoes of tension melting away, witnessed the reflections of inner stillness, and realised that within the Sands of Serenity, the boundaries between the physical and the mental were blurred—a testament to the interwoven balance of well-being.

As the sun painted the horizon with hues of gold and the pond's waters reflected the purity of the moment, Darius's journey of well-being grew more profound. He encountered meditators who found solace in the desert's embrace, engaged in conversations that celebrated the symbiotic relationship between inner and outer peace, and observed the essence of mindfulness woven into the very fabric of existence. He understood that the Sands of Serenity were not just an oasis—they were a sanctuary where the soul could find respite.

With each moment of tranquillity experienced, Darius's heart swelled with a profound sense of inner peace. He knew that the Sands of Serenity were not just a pond—they were a mirror through which one could glimpse their own balance. He realised that the bond between healer and pond was a dance of interconnected energies—a symphony of restoration and unity.

As the oasis's aura deepened and the pond's reflections seemed to hold the essence of harmony, Darius's experience gradually came to an end, leaving him before the Pond bathed in a soft, otherworldly light. He knew that the pond had granted him a gift—the ability to touch not only the water's surface but the depths of inner tranquillity.

With gratitude in his heart, Darius left the oasis and returned to his healing practice, carrying with him the insights and rejuvenation he had gained. He shared the tale of the "Sands of Serenity" and the wisdom of his holistic journey with his fellow healers and seekers of balance, reminding them that the bond between healer and pond was a dance of interconnected energies, and that the pursuit of restoring the equilibrium between body and mind and embracing the essence of well-being was a symphony of restoration and unity.

And so, dear listener, the story of Darius and the "Sands of Serenity" teaches us that inner harmony is a journey that transcends external distractions, that the bond between healer and pond is a dance of interconnected energies, and that the essence of embracing the balance between body and mind in serene retreats is a timeless truth from the heart of ancient Persia.

The Weaver's Legacy

Threads of Unity in the Heart of a Renowned Tapestry Guild

In a realm where artistic expressions united cultures and stories of craftsmanship echoed through renowned guilds, lived a young weaver named Leila. Leila's eyes held the gleam of creativity, and her heart resonated with the threads that wove societies together.

One day, as Leila explored the bustling streets of a city known for its tapestry craftsmanship, she received a vision—a vision of a hidden workshop known as the Weaver's Legacy. It was said that within the workshop's depths, the power to create tapestries that celebrated cultural diversity and embraced the essence of unity was hidden.

Intrigued by the vision, Leila ventured deeper into the city's alleys. Guided by the colours that adorned the marketplaces and the hum of conversations that celebrated various languages, she journeyed through lanes where artisans showcased their skills and workshops that seemed to hold the very soul of cultural exchange, embracing the path that artistic unity's enigma promised.

After hours of exploration, Leila arrived at a workshop where the Weaver's Legacy was said to thrive—a sanctuary of artistic craftsmanship and the connection between weaver and unity. In its centre stood the Legacy's Loom—an intricate loom adorned with symbols that seemed to reflect the interwoven nature of cultures. Leila approached the loom, and as she did, the air seemed to hum with creative energy.

With reverence, Leila took hold of the loom's shuttle and began to weave, allowing the threads to intertwine beneath her skillful touch. With each pass, she felt the heritage of diverse cultures converging, and her understanding of the world expanded. She wove threads that celebrated the motifs of various lands, witnessed patterns that echoed the stories of different societies, and realised that within the Weaver's Legacy, the boundaries between cultural differences were blurred—a testament to the interwoven fabric of human connection.

As the sunlight streamed through the workshop's windows and the loom's patterns seemed to dance with the essence of unity, Leila's artistic journey grew more profound. She encountered artisans who shared tales of their homelands' artistic traditions, observed the tapestries that resonated with universal stories, and engaged in conversations that celebrated the symbiotic relationship between art and cultural exchange. She understood that the Weaver's Legacy was not just a loom—it was a gateway through which unity was celebrated.

With each thread woven, Leila's heart swelled with a profound sense of kinship. She knew that the Weaver's Legacy was not just a workshop—it was a space where the threads of human connections were celebrated. She realised that the bond between weaver and loom was a dance of interconnected energies—a symphony of creativity and unity.

As the workshop's ambiance deepened and the loom's patterns continued their harmonious dance, Leila's artistic experience gradually came to an end, leaving her before the Loom bathed in a soft, otherworldly light. She knew that the loom had granted her a gift—the ability to weave not only threads but the harmonies of diverse cultures.

With gratitude in her heart, Leila left the workshop and returned to her artistic endeavours, carrying with her the connections and insights she had gained. She shared the tale of the "Weaver's Legacy" and the wisdom of her creative journey with her fellow weavers and seekers of artistic unity, reminding them that the bond between weaver and loom was a dance of interconnected energies, and that the pursuit of creating tapestries that celebrated cultural diversity and embraced the essence of unity was a symphony of creativity and unity.

And so, dear listener, the story of Leila and the "Weaver's Legacy" teaches us that cultural unity is a journey that transcends geographical boundaries, that the bond between weaver and loom is a dance of interconnected energies, and that the essence of embracing the threads of unity in renowned tapestry guilds is a timeless truth from the heart of ancient Persia.

The Songbird's Voyage

Melodies of Transformation in the Heart of a Mystic Garden

In a land where nature and music intertwined, and stories of transformation through song echoed through mystical gardens, lived a young songstress named Parisa. Parisa's eyes held the gleam of ambition, and her heart resonated with the enchanting power of music.

One dawn, as Parisa strolled through a lush garden adorned with exotic flora, she received a vision—a vision of a hidden grove known as the Songbird's Voyage. It was said that within the grove's heart, the power to sing melodies that connected with the spirits of nature and brought about transformation was hidden.

Intrigued by the vision, Parisa ventured deeper into the garden. Guided by the rustling leaves and the melodies of chirping birds, she journeyed through pathways where flowers seemed to sway to their own rhythm and clearings that held an aura of mystic energy, embracing the path that music's enigma promised.

After days of exploration, Parisa arrived at a grove where the Songbird's Voyage was said to thrive—a sanctuary of melodic transformation and the connection between songstress and nature. In its centre stood the Voyage's Tree—a tree adorned with intricate symbols that seemed to reflect the harmony of the natural world. Parisa approached the tree, and as she did, the air seemed to echo with harmonious resonance.

With reverence, Parisa opened her mouth and began to sing, letting her voice carry the melodies through the garden's air. With each note, she felt the presence of ancient spirits, and her understanding of the world expanded. She sang tunes that echoed the rhythms of the forest, witnessed flowers blooming in response to her melodies, and realised that within the Songbird's Voyage, the boundaries between musician and nature were blurred—a testament to the interwoven tapestry of creation.

As the sunlight filtered through the leaves and the melodies intertwined with the garden's spirit, Parisa's musical journey grew more profound. She encountered creatures that emerged from their hiding places to dance to her songs, observed the leaves rustling with a magical energy, and engaged in conversations that celebrated the symbiotic relationship between music and the natural world. She understood that the

Songbird's Voyage was not just a grove—it was a stage upon which nature's transformation through music was celebrated.

With each melodic transformation witnessed, Parisa's heart swelled with a profound sense of empowerment. She knew that the Songbird's Voyage was not just a grove—it was a portal through which her music could create change. She realised that the bond between songstress and tree was a dance of interconnected energies—a symphony of transformation and unity.

As the grove's atmosphere deepened and the tree's branches seemed to sway with the rhythm of her melodies, Parisa's experience gradually came to an end, leaving her before the Tree bathed in a soft, otherworldly light. She knew that the tree had granted her a gift—the ability to sing not only for her audience but for the very essence of nature.

With gratitude in her heart, Parisa left the grove and returned to her musical pursuits, carrying with her the transformations and insights she had gained. She shared the tale of the "Songbird's Voyage" and the wisdom of her melodic journey with her fellow songstresses and seekers of harmonious change, reminding them that the bond between musician and tree was a dance of interconnected energies, and that the pursuit of singing melodies that connected with the spirits of nature and brought about transformation was a symphony of empowerment and unity.

And so, dear listener, the story of Parisa and the "Songbird's Voyage" teaches us that music's power is a journey that transcends human audience, that the bond between musician and tree is a dance of interconnected energies, and that the essence of singing melodies that connect with the spirits of nature and bring about transformation in ancient gardens is a timeless truth from the heart of ancient Persia.

The Celestial Navigator

Guiding Stars in the Heart of a Vast Desert

In a realm where the night sky was a canvas of celestial wonders, and stories of navigation through the cosmos echoed through desert nomads, lived a young stargazer named Farid. Farid's eyes held the wonder of the universe, and his heart resonated with the mysteries of the stars.

One evening, as Farid sat beneath a sky adorned with shimmering constellations, he received a vision—a vision of a hidden sanctuary known as the Celestial Navigator's Oasis. It was said that within the oasis's heart, the power to read the stars, navigate the desert's expanse, and embrace the essence of guidance was hidden.

Intrigued by the vision, Farid embarked on a quest to find the Celestial Navigator's Oasis. Guided by the patterns of stars and the whispers of the desert winds, he journeyed through sand dunes that seemed to mirror the vastness of the cosmos and rocky formations that held an aura of wisdom, embracing the path that the desert's enigma promised.

After nights of stargazing and days of wandering, Farid arrived at an oasis where the Celestial Navigator's Oasis was said to dwell—a sanctuary of cosmic navigation and the connection between stargazer and universe. In its centre stood the Oasis's Pool—a pool adorned with intricate markings that seemed to reflect the celestial pathways. Farid approached the pool, and as he did, the air seemed to carry the resonance of celestial harmonies.

With reverence, Farid lowered his gaze into the pool's waters, observing the reflections of stars and their constellations. With each contemplative moment, he felt the universe's guidance unfolding, and his understanding of the world expanded. He read the stars' positions that foretold the desert's secrets, witnessed the patterns that pointed to hidden oases, and realised that within the Celestial Navigator's Oasis, the boundaries between the earth and the heavens were blurred—a testament to the interwoven dance of terrestrial and cosmic rhythms.

As the moonlight bathed the oasis and the pool's waters shimmered with celestial reflection, Farid's journey of navigation grew more profound. He encountered nomads who shared tales of their desert journeys guided by the stars, engaged in conversations that celebrated the connection between earthly paths and celestial maps, and observed the essence of universal guidance woven into the very fabric of existence. He understood that the Celestial Navigator's Oasis was not just a pool—it was a realm where navigation through the desert mirrored the navigation of the cosmos.

With each star chart interpreted, Farid's heart swelled with a profound sense of interconnectedness. He knew that the Celestial Navigator's Oasis was not just an oasis—it was a place where the boundaries of human and universe converged. He realised that the bond between stargazer and pool was a dance of interconnected energies—a symphony of cosmic guidance and unity.

As the oasis's ambiance deepened and the pool's reflections continued to shimmer with celestial insight, Farid's experience gradually came to an end, leaving him before the Pool bathed in a soft, otherworldly light. He knew that the pool had granted him a gift—the ability to gaze not only into its waters but into the depths of the cosmos itself.

With gratitude in his heart, Farid left the oasis and returned to his stargazing pursuits, carrying with him the guidance and insights he had gained. He shared the tale of the "Celestial Navigator" and the wisdom of his cosmic journey with his fellow stargazers and seekers of guidance, reminding them that the bond between stargazer and pool was a dance of interconnected energies, and that the pursuit of reading the stars, navigating the desert's expanse, and embracing the essence of guidance was a symphony of unity and cosmic connection.

And so, dear listener, the story of Farid and the "Celestial Navigator" teaches us that cosmic navigation is a journey that transcends the boundaries of earth, that the bond between stargazer and pool is a dance of interconnected energies, and that the essence of interpreting the stars, navigating the desert's vastness, and embracing the guidance of the universe in ancient oases is a timeless truth from the heart of ancient Persia.

The Elixir of Time

Unlocking Eternal Wisdom in the Heart of a Desert Alchemist

In a land where alchemy merged with the mysteries of existence, and stories of eternal wisdom echoed through the workshops of desert alchemists, lived a young alchemist named Azar. Azar's eyes held the gleam of curiosity, and his heart resonated with the secrets of transformation.

One dawn, as Azar conducted experiments within the walls of an ancient alchemical workshop, he received a vision—a vision of a hidden laboratory known as the Elixir of Time's Chamber. It was said that within the chamber's depths, the power to create elixirs that unlocked eternal wisdom and embraced the essence of time was hidden.

Intrigued by the vision, Azar set out to find the Elixir of Time's Chamber. Guided by the flickering flames of alchemical lamps and the whispers of ancient manuscripts, he journeyed through chambers that resonated with the echoes of arcane knowledge and corridors that seemed to pulse with the rhythm of life, embracing the path that the elixir's enigma promised.

After days of conducting experiments and deciphering texts, Azar arrived at a chamber where the Elixir of Time's Chamber was said to reside—a sanctuary of timeless wisdom and the connection between alchemist and eternity. In its centre stood the Chamber's Crucible—an intricate crucible adorned with symbols that seemed to reflect the cycles of existence. Azar approached the crucible, and as he did, the air seemed to vibrate with a mystical energy.

With reverence, Azar gathered rare ingredients and began to mix them, allowing the concoctions to react within the crucible's depths. With each reaction, he felt the currents of eternity flowing through his experiments, and his understanding of the world expanded. He mixed essences that echoed the cycles of life, witnessed transformations that held keys to eternal truths, and realised that within the Elixir of Time's Chamber, the boundaries between the finite and the infinite were blurred—a testament to the interwoven tapestry of existence.

As the alchemical lamps cast a soft glow across the chamber and the crucible's contents shimmered with a timeless luminescence, Azar's journey of unlocking wisdom grew more profound. He encountered ancient texts that foretold the nature of time's secrets, engaged in conversations that celebrated the symbiotic relationship between alchemical insights and cosmic truths, and observed the essence of universal wisdom woven into the very fabric of creation. He understood that the Elixir of Time's Chamber was not just a crucible—it was a realm where the elixirs of eternal wisdom were crafted.

With each elixir concocted, Azar's heart swelled with a profound sense of connection. He knew that the Elixir of Time's Chamber was not just a chamber—it was a space where the boundaries of human understanding merged with the cosmos.

He realised that the bond between alchemist and crucible was a dance of interconnected energies—a symphony of alchemical exploration and cosmic insight.

As the chamber's atmosphere deepened and the crucible's contents continued their timeless dance, Azar's experience gradually came to an end, leaving him before the Crucible bathed in a soft, otherworldly light. He knew that the crucible had granted him a gift—the ability to mix not only substances but the elixirs of eternal wisdom.

With gratitude in his heart, Azar left the chamber and returned to his alchemical pursuits, carrying with him the insights and eternity he had gained. He shared the tale of the "Elixir of Time" and the wisdom of his alchemical journey with his fellow alchemists and seekers of cosmic truths, reminding them that the bond between alchemist and crucible was a dance of interconnected energies, and that the pursuit of unlocking eternal wisdom and embracing the essence of time was a symphony of exploration and unity.

And so, dear listener, the story of Azar and the "Elixir of Time" teaches us that the pursuit of wisdom is a journey that transcends temporal boundaries, that the bond between alchemist and crucible is a dance of interconnected energies, and that the essence of unlocking eternal wisdom and embracing the essence of time in the workshops of desert alchemists is a timeless truth from the heart of ancient Persia.

The Silk Road Serenade

Harmony of Trade and Culture in the Heart of a Bustling Bazaar

In a realm where trade routes wove stories of exchange, and tales of cultural fusion echoed through bustling bazaars, lived a young merchant named Amir. Amir's eyes held the glint of commerce, and his heart resonated with the melodies of diverse cultures.

One market day, as Amir traversed through the stalls of a grand bazaar, he received a vision—a vision of a hidden plaza known as the Silk Road Serenade. It was said that within the plaza's heart, the power to celebrate the harmony of trade and culture through music was hidden.

Intrigued by the vision, Amir navigated deeper into the bazaar. Guided by the fragrances of exotic spices and the echoes of various languages, he journeyed through stalls where goods from distant lands converged and open spaces that held the energy of communal gatherings, embracing the path that cultural fusion's enigma promised.

After days of bartering and cultural exchanges, Amir arrived at a plaza where the Silk Road Serenade was said to come alive—a sanctuary of harmonious trade and the connection between merchant and melody. In its centre stood the Serenade's Stage—an ornate stage adorned with symbols that seemed to reflect the fusion of diverse cultures. Amir approached the stage, and as he did, the air seemed to carry the resonance of cross-cultural harmonies.

With reverence, Amir picked up a musical instrument and began to play, letting his melodies resonate through the bazaar's air. With each note, he felt the spirits of distant lands converging, and his understanding of the world expanded. He played tunes that echoed the rhythms of trade caravans, witnessed listeners from various cultures swaying to his music, and realised that within the Silk Road Serenade, the boundaries between different lands were blurred—a testament to the interwoven tapestry of global connection.

As the sun painted the plaza with hues of gold and the melodies harmonised with the market's buzz, Amir's musical journey grew more profound. He encountered traders who shared stories of their journeys across distant horizons, observed visitors from various cultures mingling to the beat of his melodies, and engaged in conversations that celebrated the symbiotic relationship between trade and cultural enrichment. He understood that the Silk Road Serenade was not just a stage—it was a platform where the fusion of commerce and culture was celebrated.

With each musical note played, Amir's heart swelled with a profound sense of unity. He knew that the Silk Road Serenade was not just a plaza—it was a space where the melodies of various cultures intertwined. He realised that the bond between merchant and stage was a dance of interconnected energies—a symphony of harmonious trade and cultural appreciation.

As the plaza's ambiance deepened and the stage's melodies continued to resonate with cross-cultural harmony, Amir's experience gradually came to an end, leaving him before the Stage bathed in a soft, otherworldly light. He knew that the stage had granted him a gift—the ability to play not only for his customers but for the very essence of cultural unity.

With gratitude in his heart, Amir left the plaza and returned to his trading ventures, carrying with him the harmonies and connections he had gained. He shared the tale of the "Silk Road Serenade" and the wisdom of his cultural journey with his fellow merchants and seekers of harmonious trade, reminding them that the bond between merchant and stage was a dance of interconnected energies, and that the pursuit of celebrating the harmony of trade and culture through music was a symphony of unity and cultural enrichment.

And so, dear listener, the story of Amir and the "Silk Road Serenade" teaches us that trade transcends the boundaries of geography, that the bond between merchant and stage is a dance of interconnected energies, and that the essence of celebrating the harmony of trade and culture through music in bustling bazaars is a timeless truth from the heart of ancient Persia.

The Secret Garden's Symphony

Harmony of Nature and Creativity in the Heart of a Mystical Garden

In a land where flora and imagination intertwined, and stories of creative inspiration echoed through hidden gardens, lived a young artist named Layla. Layla's eyes held the spark of creativity, and her heart resonated with the enchantment of the natural world.

One morning, as Layla wandered through the enchanting pathways of a mystical garden, she received a vision—a vision of a hidden glade known as the Secret Garden's Studio. It was said that within the glade's heart, the power to find artistic inspiration through nature's embrace was hidden.

Intrigued by the vision, Layla meandered deeper into the garden. Guided by the rustling leaves and the whispers of the breeze, she journeyed through flowerbeds where colours blended like an artist's palette and clearings that held an aura of creative energy, embracing the path that inspiration's enigma promised.

After days of exploration and sketching, Layla arrived at a glade where the Secret Garden's Studio was said to be found—a sanctuary of artistic inspiration and the connection between artist and nature. In its centre stood the Studio's Easel—an elaborate easel adorned with symbols that seemed to reflect the fusion of imagination and the natural world. Layla approached the easel, and as she did, the air seemed to carry the melodies of creative muse.

With reverence, Layla set up her canvas and began to paint, allowing her brushstrokes to capture the essence of the garden's beauty. With each stroke, she felt the energies of nature flowing through her creativity, and her understanding of the world expanded. She painted scenes that echoed the garden's serenity, witnessed her canvas coming alive with vibrant hues, and realised that within the Secret Garden's Studio, the boundaries between artistic expression and nature's wonders were blurred—a testament to the interwoven tapestry of creation.

As sunlight filtered through the leaves and her canvas seemed to radiate with the garden's spirit, Layla's journey of artistic inspiration grew more profound. She encountered gardeners who shared stories of their nurturing efforts, observed visitors marvelling at the fusion of nature and artistry, and engaged in conversations that celebrated the symbiotic relationship between the artist's vision and the garden's grace. She understood that the Secret Garden's Studio was not just an easel—it was a realm where the whispers of nature inspired creative masterpieces.

With each brushstroke applied, Layla's heart swelled with a profound sense of connection. She knew that the Secret Garden's Studio was not just a glade—it was a space where artistic visions were nurtured by the embrace of nature. She realised that the bond between artist and easel was a dance of interconnected energies—a symphony of creative inspiration and natural harmony.

As the glade's ambiance deepened and the easel's canvas continued to capture the garden's essence, Layla's experience gradually came to an end, leaving her before the Easel bathed in a soft, otherworldly light. She knew that the easel had granted her a gift—the ability to paint not only with pigments but with the very spirit of the garden.

With gratitude in her heart, Layla left the glade and returned to her artistic pursuits, carrying with her the inspirations and connections she had gained. She shared the tale of the "Secret Garden's Symphony" and the wisdom of her creative journey with her fellow artists and seekers of natural inspiration, reminding them that the bond between artist and easel was a dance of interconnected energies, and that the pursuit of finding artistic inspiration through nature's embrace was a symphony of creativity and natural harmony.

And so, dear listener, the story of Layla and the "Secret Garden's Symphony" teaches us that creative inspiration flows through the embrace of nature, that the bond between artist and easel is a dance of interconnected energies, and that the essence of capturing the harmony of nature and creativity in mystical gardens is a timeless truth from the heart of ancient Persia.

The Whispering Oasis

Connection to the Spirit Realm in the Heart of a Desert Sage

In a land where the desert winds carried tales of spirits, and stories of divine communion echoed through the meditations of desert sages, lived a young mystic named Nasir. Nasir's eyes held the depth of contemplation, and his heart resonated with the secrets of the unseen realm.

One twilight, as Nasir sat beneath the vast desert sky, he received a vision—a vision of a hidden oasis known as the Whispering Oasis. It was said that within the oasis's heart, the power to commune with the spirit realm and embrace the essence of spiritual connection was hidden.

Intrigued by the vision, Nasir embarked on a journey to find the Whispering Oasis. Guided by the starlit skies and the rustling sands, he journeyed through dunes that seemed to hold the echoes of ancient whispers and stone formations that carried an aura of divine presence, embracing the path that spiritual communion's enigma promised.

After nights of meditation and soul-searching, Nasir arrived at an oasis where the Whispering Oasis was said to reside—a sanctuary of ethereal connection and the bond between mystic and spirits. In its centre stood the Oasis's Pool—an enigmatic pool adorned with symbols that seemed to reflect the dance between the seen and the unseen. Nasir approached the pool, and as he did, the air seemed to carry the resonance of spiritual harmony.

With reverence, Nasir knelt by the pool's edge and began to meditate, allowing his mind to transcend the physical realm and connect with the spirit realm. With each breath, he felt the presence of ancient souls surrounding him, and his understanding of the world expanded.

He communed with spirits that whispered tales of bygone eras, witnessed his consciousness merging with the tapestry of eternity, and realised that within the Whispering Oasis, the boundaries between the mortal and the divine were blurred—a testament to the interwoven dance of existence.

As the moon cast a silvery glow across the oasis and Nasir's meditative state deepened, his journey of spiritual connection grew more profound. He encountered fellow seekers who shared visions of their encounters with the spirit realm, engaged in conversations that celebrated the symbiotic relationship between the mortal and the eternal, and observed the essence of ethereal harmony woven into the very fabric of the cosmos. He understood that the Whispering Oasis was not just a pool—it was a gateway to commune with the spirits.

With each moment of spiritual communion, Nasir's heart swelled with a profound sense of unity. He knew that the Whispering Oasis was not just an oasis—it was a realm where the barriers between the living and the departed dissolved. He realised that the bond between mystic and pool was a dance of interconnected energies—a symphony of divine connection and spiritual embrace.

As the oasis's aura deepened and the pool's surface seemed to ripple with celestial wisdom, Nasir's experience gradually came to an end, leaving him before the Pool bathed in a soft, otherworldly light. He knew that the pool had granted him a gift—the ability to meditate not only for his own consciousness but for the communion of souls.

With gratitude in his heart, Nasir left the oasis and returned to his meditative practices, carrying with him the connections and insights he had gained. He shared the tale of the "Whispering Oasis" and the wisdom of his spiritual journey with his fellow seekers of divine communion, reminding them that the bond between mystic and pool was a dance of interconnected energies, and that the pursuit of communing with the spirit realm and embracing the essence of spiritual connection was a symphony of unity and ethereal harmony.

And so, dear listener, the story of Nasir and the "Whispering Oasis" teaches us that spiritual connection transcends the boundaries of the seen, that the bond between mystic and pool is a dance of interconnected energies, and that the essence of communing with the spirit realm and embracing the essence of spiritual connection in the meditations of desert sages is a timeless truth from the heart of ancient Persia.

The Labyrinth of Wisdom

Journey of Enlightenment in the Heart of a Mysterious Maze

In a realm where knowledge and mystery intertwined, and stories of spiritual enlightenment echoed through ancient labyrinths, lived a young scholar named Zara. Zara's eyes held the spark of curiosity, and her heart resonated with the pursuit of profound wisdom.

One morning, as Zara wandered through the corridors of a labyrinthine structure, she received a vision—a vision of a hidden chamber known as the Labyrinth of Wisdom's Sanctuary. It was said that within the chamber's heart, the power to gain enlightenment through navigating the labyrinth was hidden.

Intrigued by the vision, Zara ventured deeper into the labyrinth. Guided by the twists and turns that seemed to hold the essence of the journey itself, she journeyed through passageways that resonated with the echoes of ancient teachings and chambers that held an aura of hidden truths, embracing the path that enlightenment's enigma promised.

After days of exploration and contemplation, Zara arrived at a chamber where the Labyrinth of Wisdom's Sanctuary was said to dwell—a sanctuary of spiritual illumination and the connection between seeker and labyrinth. In its centre stood the Sanctuary's Altar—an intricate altar adorned with symbols that seemed to reflect the dance of knowledge and understanding. Zara approached the altar, and as she did, the air seemed to carry the resonance of sacred insight.

With reverence, Zara sat before the altar and began to meditate, allowing her mind to navigate the labyrinth of her thoughts and gain enlightenment through inner exploration. With each introspective moment, she felt the currents of wisdom flowing through her consciousness, and her understanding of the world expanded. She navigated mental corridors that echoed the lessons of ancient sages, witnessed the chambers of her mind unveiling profound truths, and realised that within the Labyrinth of Wisdom's Sanctuary, the boundaries between seeker and labyrinth were blurred—a testament to the interwoven tapestry of inner and outer journeys.

As sunlight streamed through openings in the labyrinth's walls and Zara's meditation deepened, her journey of enlightenment grew more profound. She encountered seekers who shared insights gained from traversing their inner labyrinths, engaged in conversations that

celebrated the symbiotic relationship between personal growth and the pursuit of wisdom, and observed the essence of universal truth woven into the very fabric of existence.
She understood that the Labyrinth of Wisdom's Sanctuary was not just an altar—it was a space where the pathways of thought converged with the journey of self-discovery.

With each moment of insight gained, Zara's heart swelled with a profound sense of interconnectedness. She knew that the Labyrinth of Wisdom's Sanctuary was not just a chamber—it was a realm where seeker and labyrinth merged. She realised that the bond between seeker and altar was a dance of interconnected energies—a symphony of enlightenment and self-realisation.

As the chamber's ambiance deepened and the altar's symbols seemed to glow with inner light, Zara's experience gradually came to an end, leaving her before the Altar bathed in a soft, otherworldly light. She knew that the altar had granted her a gift—the ability to meditate not only for the illumination of her own mind but for the connection between inner and outer journeys.

With gratitude in her heart, Zara left the chamber and returned to her scholarly pursuits, carrying with her the insights and enlightenment she had gained.

 She shared the tale of the "Labyrinth of Wisdom" and the wisdom of her introspective journey with her fellow seekers of profound truths, reminding them that the bond between seeker and altar was a dance of interconnected energies, and that the pursuit of gaining enlightenment through navigating the labyrinth of inner thoughts was a symphony of unity and personal growth.

And so, dear listener, the story of Zara and the "Labyrinth of Wisdom" teaches us that enlightenment transcends the boundaries of physical space, that the bond between seeker and altar is a dance of interconnected energies, and that the essence of gaining insight and understanding through navigating the labyrinth of inner thoughts in ancient mazes is a timeless truth from the heart of ancient Persia.

The Phoenix's Riddle

Eternal Rebirth in the Heart of a Desert Enigma

In a land where myths and mysteries intertwined, and stories of eternal renewal echoed through desert winds, lived a young adventurer named Azra. Azra's eyes held the spark of curiosity, and her heart resonated with the secrets of rebirth.

One day, as Azra explored the arid landscapes of the desert, she received a vision—a vision of a hidden oasis known as the Phoenix's Oasis. It was said that within the oasis's heart, the power to solve the riddle of the phoenix and embrace the essence of eternal renewal was hidden.

Intrigued by the vision, Azra embarked on a quest to find the Phoenix's Oasis. Guided by the shifting sands and the echoes of distant cries, she journeyed through dunes that seemed to carry the echoes of the phoenix's song and rocky formations that held an aura of ancient wisdom, embracing the path that the riddle's enigma promised.

After days of deciphering ancient texts and observing the patterns of the desert, Azra arrived at an oasis where the Phoenix's Oasis was said to reside—a sanctuary of eternal rebirth and the connection between seeker and phoenix.
In its centre stood the Oasis's Fountain—an elaborate fountain adorned with symbols that seemed to reflect the dance of life and death. Azra approached the fountain, and as she did, the air seemed to carry the resonance of the phoenix's cry.

With reverence, Azra studied the symbols and contemplated the riddle of the phoenix—an enigma that had perplexed generations. She delved into the lore of the phoenix's cycles of death and rebirth, witnessing the patterns of nature's eternal rhythm, and realised that within the Phoenix's Oasis, the boundaries between life and death were blurred—a testament to the interwoven tapestry of renewal.

As the sun painted the oasis with shades of amber and the fountain's waters shimmered with a golden glow, Azra's journey of deciphering the riddle grew more profound. She encountered scholars who shared their interpretations of the phoenix's enigma, engaged in conversations that celebrated the symbiotic relationship between the phoenix's cycles and the seasons, and observed the essence of eternal renewal woven into the very fabric of existence. She understood that the Phoenix's Oasis was not just a fountain—it was a realm where the phoenix's riddle revealed the secrets of rebirth.

With each contemplative moment, Azra's heart swelled with a profound sense of connection. She knew that the Phoenix's Oasis was not just an oasis—it was a space where the phoenix's cry echoed through time. She realised that the bond between seeker and fountain was a dance of interconnected energies—a symphony of enigma and eternal renewal.

As the oasis's aura deepened and the fountain's waters continued to ripple with mysteries, Azra's experience gradually came to an end, leaving her before the Fountain bathed in a soft, otherworldly light. She knew that the fountain had granted her a gift—the ability to ponder not only the riddle but the cycles of rebirth itself.
With gratitude in her heart, Azra left the oasis and returned to her explorations, carrying with her the insights and connections she had gained. She shared the tale of the "Phoenix's Riddle" and the wisdom of her quest with her fellow seekers of ancient secrets, reminding them that the bond between seeker and fountain was a dance of interconnected energies, and that the pursuit of solving the riddle of the phoenix and embracing the essence of eternal renewal was a symphony of unity and mystery.

And so, dear listener, the story of Azra and the "Phoenix's Riddle" teaches us that the phoenix's cycle transcends the boundaries of mortality, that the bond between seeker and fountain is a dance of interconnected energies, and that the essence of solving the riddle of eternal rebirth in the heart of a desert enigma is a timeless truth from the heart of ancient Persia.

The Artisan's Mirage

Reflection of Creation in the Heart of a Desert Sculptor

In a realm where artistic mastery and illusions intertwined, and stories of extraordinary craftsmanship echoed through desert communities, lived a young sculptor named Farhad. Farhad's eyes held the gleam of creativity, and his heart resonated with the allure of transformation.

One morning, as Farhad chiselled away at a block of stone within his humble workshop, he received a vision—a vision of a hidden cavern known as the Artisan's Grotto. It was said that within the grotto's heart, the power to sculpt illusions that reflected the essence of creation was hidden.

Intrigued by the vision, Farhad ventured into the desert's expanse. Guided by the shifting shadows and the whispers of the wind, he journeyed through canyons that seemed to hold the echoes of unseen worlds and sand formations that carried an aura of artistic inspiration, embracing the path that the illusion's enigma promised.

After days of sculpting and experimenting, Farhad arrived at a cavern where the Artisan's Grotto was said to be found—a sanctuary of creative illusion and the connection between sculptor and vision. In its centre stood the Grotto's Easel—a magnificent easel adorned with symbols that seemed to reflect the convergence of reality and imagination. Farhad approached the easel, and as he did, the air seemed to shimmer with artistic resonance.

With reverence, Farhad picked up his tools and began to sculpt, allowing his hands to shape illusions that transcended the boundaries of the material world. With each carving, he felt the flow of creativity coursing through his veins, and his understanding of the world expanded. He sculpted forms that seemed to merge the tangible with the intangible, witnessed the outlines of existence bending under his artistic touch, and realised that within the Artisan's Grotto, the boundaries between the finite and the infinite were blurred—a testament to the interwoven dance of artistic expression and reality.

As the desert's sun cast shifting patterns of light across the grotto's walls and Farhad's illusions took on a life of their own, his journey of sculpting illusions grew more profound. He encountered fellow artisans who shared stories of their creations coming to life, engaged in conversations that celebrated the symbiotic relationship between artistic vision and tangible forms, and observed the essence of creative mastery woven into the very fabric of the universe. He understood that the Artisan's Grotto was not just an easel—it was a realm where illusions reflected the tapestry of creation.

With each illusion sculpted, Farhad's heart swelled with a profound sense of unity. He knew that the Artisan's Grotto was not just a cavern—it was a space where the artist's touch reshaped reality. He realised that the bond between sculptor and easel was a dance of interconnected energies—a symphony of creative expression and the convergence of realms.

As the grotto's ambiance deepened and the easel's forms seemed to shift and transform, Farhad's experience gradually came to an end, leaving him before the Easel bathed in a soft, otherworldly light. He knew that the easel had granted him a gift—the ability to sculpt not only with his hands but with the very essence of creation.

With gratitude in his heart, Farhad left the grotto and returned to his sculpting endeavours, carrying with him the illusions and insights he had gained. He shared the tale of the "Artisan's Mirage" and the wisdom of his creative journey with his fellow craftsmen and seekers of artistic transcendence, reminding them that the bond between sculptor and easel was a dance of interconnected energies, and that the pursuit of sculpting illusions that reflected the essence of creation was a symphony of unity and transformation.

And so, dear listener, the story of Farhad and the "Artisan's Mirage" teaches us that artistic expression transcends the boundaries of the tangible, that the bond between sculptor and easel is a dance of interconnected energies, and that the essence of sculpting illusions that reflect the essence of creation within the heart of a desert sculptor's grotto is a timeless truth from the heart of ancient Persia.

The Enchanted Mirror

Portal to Other Realms in the Heart of a Mysterious Glassworker

In a land where craftsmanship and magic intertwined, and stories of mystical portals echoed through glassblower's workshops, lived a young artisan named Leila. Leila's eyes held the shimmer of wonder, and her heart resonated with the allure of hidden dimensions.

One evening, as Leila shaped molten glass into delicate forms within her workshop, she received a vision—a vision of a hidden chamber known as the Enchanted Atelier. It was said that within the atelier's heart, the power to craft mirrors that served as portals to other realms was hidden.

Intrigued by the vision, Leila set out to find the Enchanted Atelier. Guided by the flickering flames and the whispers of the wind, she journeyed through glassblowing workshops that seemed to hold the secrets of the unseen and reflections that carried an aura of mystery, embracing the path that the mirror's enigma promised.

After days of experimentation and study, Leila arrived at a chamber where the Enchanted Atelier was said to reside—a sanctuary of magical portals and the connection between artisan and mirror. In its centre stood the Atelier's Mirror—an ornate mirror adorned with symbols that seemed to reflect the dance of worlds. Leila approached the mirror, and as she did, the air seemed to shimmer with enchantment.

With reverence, Leila began to work on the mirror's frame, carefully crafting intricate patterns that resonated with the magic she felt within the atelier.

With each stroke of her tools, she felt the weave of mysticism intertwining with her craftsmanship, and her understanding of the world expanded. She decorated the mirror's surface with designs that seemed to come alive, witnessed the mirror's reflection bending and distorting reality, and realised that within the Enchanted Atelier, the boundaries between the mundane and the magical were blurred—a testament to the interwoven dance of craft and enchantment.

As candlelight danced across the atelier's walls and the mirror's surface seemed to ripple with hidden energies, Leila's journey of crafting magical mirrors grew more profound. She encountered fellow glassworkers who shared tales of their own journeys into other realms through their creations, engaged in conversations that celebrated the symbiotic relationship between artistry and the mystical, and observed the essence of portal magic woven into the very fabric of existence. She understood that the Enchanted Atelier was not just a chamber—it was a realm where mirrors held the keys to other worlds.

With each delicate stroke on the mirror's frame, Leila's heart swelled with a profound sense of unity. She knew that the Enchanted Atelier was not just a place—it was a space where reflections defied the laws of reality. She realised that the bond between artisan and mirror was a dance of interconnected energies—a symphony of magic and craftsmanship.

As the atelier's ambiance deepened and the mirror's surface seemed to glow with ethereal light, Leila's experience gradually came to an end, leaving her before the Mirror bathed in a soft, otherworldly glow. She knew that the mirror had granted her a gift—the ability to craft not only with her hands but with the very essence of other realms.

With gratitude in her heart, Leila left the atelier and returned to her glassblowing pursuits, carrying with her the enchantments and connections she had gained. She shared the tale of the "Enchanted Mirror" and the wisdom of her mystical journey with her fellow artisans and seekers of hidden dimensions, reminding them that the bond between artisan and mirror was a dance of interconnected energies, and that the pursuit of crafting mirrors that served as portals to other realms was a symphony of unity and enchantment.

And so, dear listener, the story of Leila and the "Enchanted Mirror" teaches us that mystical portals transcend the boundaries of the seen, that the bond between artisan and mirror is a dance of interconnected energies, and that the essence of crafting mirrors that serve as portals to other realms within the heart of a mysterious glassworker's atelier is a timeless truth from the heart of ancient Persia.

The Astral Weaver

Interstellar Tapestry in the Heart of a Celestial Seamstress

In a realm where constellations and creativity intertwined, and stories of cosmic artistry echoed through observatories, lived a young seamstress named Amina. Amina's eyes held the glimmer of stardust, and her heart resonated with the wonders of the universe.

One night, as Amina worked on a celestial-themed tapestry within her modest studio, she received a vision—a vision of a hidden chamber known as the Astral Atelier.
 It was said that within the atelier's heart, the power to weave fabrics that connected to the cosmos was hidden.

Intrigued by the vision, Amina embarked on a journey to find the Astral Atelier. Guided by the shimmering stars and the whispers of cosmic winds, she journeyed through observatories that seemed to hold the secrets of the galaxies and fabrics that carried an aura of interstellar beauty, embracing the path that the tapestry's enigma promised.

After days of studying celestial patterns and perfecting her craft, Amina arrived at a chamber where the Astral Atelier was said to reside—a sanctuary of cosmic tapestries and the connection between weaver and universe. In its centre stood the Atelier's Loom—an intricate loom adorned with symbols that seemed to reflect the dance of stars and threads. Amina approached the loom, and as she did, the air seemed to hum with celestial resonance.

With reverence, Amina began to weave, allowing her fingers to intertwine threads that echoed the constellations above. With each stroke of her hands, she felt the energies of the cosmos flowing through her creations, and her understanding of the world expanded. She wove patterns that seemed to bridge the realms of Earth and sky, witnessed her tapestries coming alive with celestial radiance, and realised that within the Astral Atelier, the boundaries between the terrestrial and the celestial were blurred—a testament to the interwoven dance of craft and cosmic connection.

As moonlight bathed the atelier's surroundings and Amina's tapestries glowed with otherworldly light, her journey of weaving cosmic fabrics grew more profound. She encountered fellow weavers who shared tales of their tapestries resonating with the energies of the stars, engaged in conversations that celebrated the symbiotic relationship between artistry and the cosmos, and observed the essence of universal harmony woven into the very fabric of existence. She understood that the Astral Atelier was not just a chamber—it was a realm where the threads of the universe converged with the threads of her tapestries.

With each delicate weave, Amina's heart swelled with a profound sense of unity. She knew that the Astral Atelier was not just a place—it was a space where the universe's patterns manifested through her craft. She realised that the bond between weaver and loom was a dance of interconnected energies—a symphony of cosmic artistry and celestial resonance.

As the atelier's ambiance deepened and the tapestries' radiance seemed to reflect the stars themselves, Amina's experience gradually came to an end, leaving her before the Loom bathed in a soft, otherworldly glow. She knew that the loom had granted her a gift—the ability to weave not only with her hands but with the very essence of the universe.

With gratitude in her heart, Amina left the atelier and returned to her tapestry weaving, carrying with her the cosmic fabrics and insights she had gained. She shared the tale of the "Astral Weaver" and the wisdom of her interstellar journey with her fellow artisans and seekers of cosmic beauty, reminding them that the bond between weaver and loom was a dance of interconnected energies, and that the pursuit of weaving fabrics that connected to the cosmos was a symphony of unity and celestial artistry.

And so, dear listener, the story of Amina and the "Astral Weaver" teaches us that cosmic connection transcends the boundaries of the Earthly, that the bond between weaver and loom is a dance of interconnected energies, and that the essence of weaving fabrics that reflect the wonders of the universe within the heart of a celestial seamstress's atelier is a timeless truth from the heart of ancient Persia.

The Nomad's Melody

Harmony of Cultures in the Heart of a Travelling Musician

In a land where melodies and traditions intertwined, and stories of cross-cultural harmony echoed through the paths of nomads, lived a young musician named Arman. Arman's eyes held the twinkle of adventure, and his heart resonated with the symphony of diverse cultures.

One evening, as Arman played his melodies beneath the desert stars, he received a vision—a vision of a hidden gathering known as the Nomad's Encampment. It was said that within the encampment's heart, the power to compose harmonies that celebrated cultural diversity was hidden.

Intrigued by the vision, Arman embarked on a journey to find the Nomad's Encampment. Guided by the echoes of distant songs and the footprints left by nomadic tribes, he journeyed through landscapes that seemed to carry the spirit of unity and traditions that held an aura of shared wisdom, embracing the path that the harmony's enigma promised.

After days of learning traditional tunes and absorbing the stories of diverse cultures, Arman arrived at a gathering where the Nomad's Encampment was said to be held—a sanctuary of cross-cultural melodies and the connection between musician and world. In its centre stood the Encampment's Bonfire—an inviting bonfire adorned with symbols that seemed to reflect the dance of different cultures. Arman approached the bonfire, and as he did, the air seemed to resonate with the vibrations of countless harmonies.

With reverence, Arman began to play his melodies, allowing his fingers to weave together tunes that celebrated the essence of cultural diversity. With each note, he felt the unity of humanity flowing through his compositions, and his understanding of the world expanded. He played harmonies that merged the melodies of faraway lands, witnessed the bonfire's flames dancing in rhythm to his music, and realised that within the Nomad's Encampment, the boundaries between different cultures were blurred—a testament to the interwoven dance of music and unity.

As moonlight bathed the encampment's grounds and Arman's melodies resonated with a sense of shared humanity, his journey of composing cross-cultural harmonies grew more profound. He encountered fellow musicians who shared their own interpretations of melodies from distant lands, engaged in conversations that celebrated the symbiotic relationship between music and cultural understanding, and observed the essence of universal harmony woven into the very fabric of societies.

He understood that the Nomad's Encampment was not just a gathering—it was a realm where melodies bridged the gaps between different worlds.

With each harmonious chord struck, Arman's heart swelled with a profound sense of connection. He knew that the Nomad's Encampment was not just a place—it was a space where the echoes of diverse cultures merged into one melody. He realised that the bond between musician and bonfire was a dance of interconnected energies—a symphony of cross-cultural understanding and shared harmony.

As the encampment's ambiance deepened and the bonfire's flames seemed to dance with the melodies themselves, Arman's experience gradually came to an end, leaving him before the Bonfire bathed in a soft, otherworldly glow. He knew that the bonfire had granted him a gift—the ability to compose not only with his instrument but with the very essence of cultural unity.

With gratitude in his heart, Arman left the encampment and returned to his musical endeavours, carrying with him the melodies and connections he had gained. He shared the tale of the "Nomad's Melody" and the wisdom of his cross-cultural journey with his fellow musicians and seekers of harmonious understanding, reminding them that the bond between musician and bonfire was a dance of interconnected energies, and that the pursuit of composing harmonies that celebrated cultural diversity was a symphony of unity and shared melodies.

And so, dear listener, the story of Arman and the "Nomad's Melody" teaches us that cultural harmony transcends the boundaries of distance, that the bond between musician and bonfire is a dance of interconnected energies, and that the essence of composing harmonies that celebrate the unity of different cultures within the heart of a travelling musician's encampment is a timeless truth from the heart of ancient Persia.

The Oracle's Veil

Visions of Fate in the Heart of a Mysterious Seer

In a realm where prophecies and enigma intertwined, and stories of fate's whispers echoed through ancient temples, lived a mysterious seer named Kasra. Kasra's eyes held the depth of foresight, and his heart resonated with the secrets of destiny.

One twilight, as Kasra gazed into his scrying bowl within his secluded chamber, he received a vision—a vision of a hidden sanctuary known as the Oracle's Sanctum. It was said that within the sanctum's heart, the power to unveil the mysteries of fate was hidden.

Intrigued by the vision, Kasra embarked on a quest to find the Oracle's Sanctum. Guided by the moon's glow and the rustling leaves, he journeyed through forests that seemed to hold the echoes of time and ruins that carried an aura of ancient wisdom, embracing the path that the oracle's enigma promised.

After days of deciphering cryptic symbols and delving into the lore of fate, Kasra arrived at a sanctuary where the Oracle's Sanctum was said to reside—a realm of divine visions and the connection between seer and destiny. In its centre stood the Sanctum's Veil—a magnificent veil adorned with symbols that seemed to reflect the ebb and flow of life's currents. Kasra approached the veil, and as he did, the air seemed to tremble with the whispers of the unknown.

With reverence, Kasra closed his eyes and focused his mind, allowing his inner visions to weave the tapestry of destiny. With each breath, he felt the threads of fate intertwining with his consciousness, and his understanding of the world expanded. He witnessed the tapestry of lives and events unfurling before him, saw the paths of individuals and nations converging and diverging, and realised that within the Oracle's Sanctum, the boundaries between past, present, and future were blurred—a testament to the interwoven dance of foresight and time.

As starlight filtered through the sanctum's openings and Kasra's visions revealed hidden truths, his journey of deciphering fate's enigmas grew more profound. He encountered fellow seers who shared their insights into the threads of destiny, engaged in conversations that celebrated the symbiotic relationship between prophecy and choice, and observed the essence of cosmic order woven into the very fabric of existence. He understood that the Oracle's Sanctum was not just a sanctuary—it was a realm where the veils of time were lifted.

With each revealed vision, Kasra's heart swelled with a profound sense of unity. He knew that the Oracle's Sanctum was not just a place—it was a space where the tapestry of fate was woven. He realised that the bond between seer and veil was a dance of interconnected energies—a symphony of visions and the flow of destiny.

As the sanctum's ambiance deepened and the veil's symbols seemed to shimmer with ethereal light, Kasra's experience gradually came to an end, leaving him before the Veil bathed in a soft, otherworldly glow. He knew that the veil had granted him a gift—the ability to peer not only into his scrying bowl but into the very fabric of time.

With gratitude in his heart, Kasra left the sanctum and returned to his seer's duties, carrying with him the visions and insights he had gained. He shared the tale of the "Oracle's Veil" and the wisdom of his journey with his fellow seekers of destiny, reminding them that the bond between seer and veil was a dance of interconnected energies, and that the pursuit of unveiling the mysteries of fate within the heart of a mysterious seer's sanctuary was a symphony of unity and cosmic insight.

And so, dear listener, the story of Kasra and the "Oracle's Veil" teaches us that destiny transcends the boundaries of time, that the bond between seer and veil is a dance of interconnected energies, and that the essence of unravelling the tapestry of fate within the heart of a mysterious seer's sanctuary is a timeless truth from the heart of ancient Persia.

The Celestial Navigator

Guidance from the Stars in the Heart of an Astral Voyager

In a land where celestial maps and exploration intertwined, and stories of navigational prowess echoed through astronomer's observatories, lived a young stargazer named Armina. Armina's eyes held the spark of curiosity, and her heart resonated with the mysteries of the cosmos.

One night, as Armina charted constellations within her observatory, she received a vision—a vision of a hidden chamber known as the Celestial Vault. It was said that within the vault's heart, the power to navigate by the stars and uncover astral secrets was hidden.

Intrigued by the vision, Armina set out to find the Celestial Vault. Guided by the shimmering constellations and the whispers of the night sky, she journeyed through dark forests that seemed to hold the echoes of starlight and skyward paths that carried an aura of cosmic wisdom, embracing the path that the navigation's enigma promised.

After days of studying celestial patterns and honing her skills, Armina arrived at a chamber where the Celestial Vault was said to reside—a sanctuary of astral maps and the connection between navigator and cosmos. In its centre stood the Vault's Astrolabe—an intricate astrolabe adorned with symbols that seemed to reflect the dance of planets and stars. Armina approached the astrolabe, and as she did, the air seemed to vibrate with the echoes of distant galaxies.

With reverence, Armina manipulated the astrolabe's arms, aligning it with the constellations above and below. With each adjustment, she felt the pulse of the universe synchronising with her intent, and her understanding of the world expanded.

She plotted courses that led to distant celestial bodies, witnessed the astrolabe's symbols merging with the patterns of the night sky, and realised that within the Celestial Vault, the boundaries between the terrestrial and the celestial were blurred—a testament to the interwoven dance of exploration and starlight.

As moonlight bathed the vault's surroundings and Armina's navigational maps took on an ethereal glow, her journey of charting astral courses grew more profound. She encountered fellow astronomers who shared their insights into navigating by the stars, engaged in conversations that celebrated the symbiotic relationship between discovery and the cosmos, and observed the essence of cosmic order woven into the very fabric of the heavens. She understood that the Celestial Vault was not just a chamber—it was a realm where navigators harmonised their paths with the cosmos.

With each plotted course, Armina's heart swelled with a profound sense of connection. She knew that the Celestial Vault was not just a place—it was a space where the navigator's intent intertwined with the universe's will. She realised that the bond between navigator and astrolabe was a dance of interconnected energies—a symphony of exploration and celestial alignment.

As the vault's ambiance deepened and the astrolabe's symbols seemed to gleam with starlit brilliance, Armina's experience gradually came to an end, leaving her before the Astrolabe bathed in a soft, otherworldly light. She knew that the astrolabe had granted her a gift—the ability to navigate not only the Earth but the vast expanse of the cosmos.

With gratitude in her heart, Armina left the vault and returned to her stargazing pursuits, carrying with her the astral maps and insights she had gained. She shared the tale of the "Celestial Navigator" and the wisdom of her astral journey with her fellow stargazers and seekers of cosmic understanding, reminding them that the bond between navigator and astrolabe was a dance of interconnected energies, and that the pursuit of charting courses by the stars within the heart of an astral voyager's sanctuary was a symphony of unity and celestial exploration.

And so, dear listener, the story of Armina and the "Celestial Navigator" teaches us that cosmic guidance transcends the boundaries of the Earthly, that the bond between navigator and astrolabe is a dance of interconnected energies, and that the essence of charting astral courses within the heart of an astral voyager's sanctuary is a timeless truth from the heart of ancient Persia.

The Enchanted Oasis

Mirage of Miracles in the Heart of a Seeker

In a desert land where tales of enchantment and the lure of the unknown intertwined, lived a wanderer named Farid. Farid's eyes held the glint of adventure, and his heart resonated with the promise of miracles.

One day, as Farid journeyed through the vast dunes and shimmering heat, he received a vision—a vision of an oasis known as the Enchanted Oasis. It was said that within the oasis's heart, the power to manifest desires and witness mirages of wonder was hidden.

Intrigued by the vision, Farid embarked on a quest to find the Enchanted Oasis. Guided by the dancing mirages and the whispers of the desert winds, he journeyed through shifting sands that seemed to hold secrets and distant horizons that carried an aura of magic, embracing the path that the oasis's enigma promised.

After days of venturing through the desert and tapping into his inner yearnings, Farid arrived at an oasis where the Enchanted Oasis was said to reside—a sanctuary of shimmering waters and the connection between seeker and mirage. In its centre stood the Oasis's Spring—an inviting spring adorned with symbols that seemed to reflect the dance of dreams and illusions. Farid approached the spring, and as he did, the air seemed to quiver with the vibrations of desire.

With reverence, Farid gazed into the spring's waters, allowing his deepest wishes and aspirations to rise to the surface. With each reflection, he felt the pulse of his desires resonating with the energies of the oasis, and his understanding of the world expanded. He witnessed mirages of his dreams manifesting before him, saw the oasis's waters shimmering with ethereal light, and realised that within the Enchanted Oasis, the boundaries between reality and imagination were blurred—a testament to the interwoven dance of yearning and manifestation.

As the sun's rays danced upon the oasis's surface and Farid's visions took on a life of their own, his journey of exploring the realm of desires grew more profound. He encountered fellow seekers who shared their own experiences of mirages and dreams coming true, engaged in conversations that celebrated the symbiotic relationship between intention and reality, and observed the essence of the human spirit's potential woven into the very fabric of existence. He understood that the

Enchanted Oasis was not just a location—it was a realm where the whispers of the heart were heard.

With each fulfilled vision, Farid's heart swelled with a profound sense of unity. He knew that the Enchanted Oasis was not just a place—it was a space where desires and reality intertwined. He realised that the bond between seeker and spring was a dance of interconnected energies—a symphony of manifestation and the call of the heart.

As the oasis's ambiance deepened and the spring's waters seemed to glow with inner radiance, Farid's experience gradually came to an end, leaving him before the Spring bathed in a soft, otherworldly light. He knew that the spring had granted him a gift—the ability to tap not only into his inner yearnings but into the very currents of desire.

With gratitude in his heart, Farid left the oasis and continued his wanderings, carrying with him the enchanted visions and insights he had gained. He shared the tale of the "Enchanted Oasis" and the wisdom of his journey with his fellow seekers of miracles, reminding them that the bond between seeker and spring was a dance of interconnected energies, and that the pursuit of manifesting desires within the heart of an enchanted seeker's sanctuary was a symphony of unity and wonder.

And so, dear listener, the story of Farid and the "Enchanted Oasis" teaches us that miracles transcend the boundaries of reality, that the bond between seeker and spring is a dance of interconnected energies, and that the essence of manifesting desires within the heart of an enchanted seeker's sanctuary is a timeless truth from the heart of ancient Persia.

The Celestial Sculptor

Whispers of the Stars in the Heart of a Cosmic Craftsman

In a realm where sculptures and celestial beauty intertwined, and stories of creative inspiration echoed through artist's workshops, lived a young sculptor named Ramin. Ramin's eyes held the gleam of imagination, and his heart resonated with the mysteries of the cosmos.

One evening, as Ramin chiselled away at a marble block within his workshop, he received a vision—a vision of a hidden grotto known as the Celestial Atelier. It was said that within the atelier's heart, the power to sculpt illusions that captured the essence of the stars was hidden.

Intrigued by the vision, Ramin set out to find the Celestial Atelier. Guided by the patterns of constellations and the whispers of the night breeze, he journeyed through moonlit valleys that seemed to echo with creative secrets and skyward paths that carried an aura of cosmic wonder, embracing the path that the atelier's enigma promised.

After days of studying the heavens and honing his sculpting skills, Ramin arrived at a grotto where the Celestial Atelier was said to reside—a sanctuary of celestial sculptures and the connection between sculptor and cosmos.

In its centre stood the Atelier's Easel—an exquisite easel adorned with symbols that seemed to reflect the dance of galaxies and stars. Ramin approached the easel, and as he did, the air seemed to shimmer with cosmic energy.

With reverence, Ramin picked up his sculpting tools and began to carve away at the marble, allowing his imagination to blend with the mysteries of the stars. With each stroke of his tools, he felt the energies of the cosmos guiding his hands, and his understanding of the world expanded. He sculpted illusions that captured the essence of nebulae and galaxies, witnessed his sculptures coming to life with celestial radiance, and realised that within the Celestial Atelier, the boundaries between the earthly and the cosmic were blurred—a testament to the interwoven dance of artistic inspiration and the allure of the universe.

As starlight bathed the grotto's walls and Ramin's sculptures gleamed with ethereal light, his journey of sculpting celestial forms grew more profound. He encountered fellow artists who shared their own interpretations of cosmic beauty, engaged in conversations that celebrated the symbiotic relationship between creativity and the cosmos, and observed the essence of cosmic harmony woven into the very fabric of existence. He understood that the Celestial Atelier was not just a grotto—it was a realm where artists fused their visions with the stars.

With each sculpted illusion, Ramin's heart swelled with a profound sense of connection. He knew that the Celestial Atelier was not just a place—it was a space where sculptures mirrored the cosmos. He realised that the bond between sculptor and easel was a dance of interconnected energies—a symphony of creative expression and celestial inspiration.

As the grotto's ambiance deepened and the easel's symbols seemed to radiate with
cosmic brilliance, Ramin's experience gradually came to an end, leaving him before the Easel bathed in a soft, otherworldly radiance. He knew that the easel had granted him a gift—the ability to sculpt not only with his hands but with the very essence of the stars.

With gratitude in his heart, Ramin left the grotto and returned to his sculpting endeavours, carrying with him the celestial sculptures and insights he had gained. He shared the tale of the "Celestial Sculptor" and the wisdom of his cosmic journey with his fellow artists and seekers of artistic inspiration, reminding them that the bond between sculptor and easel was a dance of interconnected energies, and that the pursuit of sculpting illusions that captured the essence of the stars within the heart of a cosmic craftsman's atelier was a symphony of unity and cosmic artistry.

And so, dear listener, the story of Ramin and the "Celestial Sculptor" teaches us that cosmic inspiration transcends the boundaries of Earthly limitations, that the bond between sculptor and easel is a dance of interconnected energies, and that the essence of sculpting celestial illusions within the heart of a cosmic craftsman's atelier is a timeless truth from the heart of ancient Persia.

The Chalice of Wisdom

Reflections of Knowledge in the Heart of a Scholar

In a land where scrolls and intellectual pursuits intertwined, and stories of the pursuit of knowledge echoed through the halls of ancient libraries, lived a dedicated scholar named Parisa. Parisa's eyes held the gleam of curiosity, and her heart resonated with the mysteries of wisdom.

One day, as Parisa delved into ancient texts within the archives, she received a vision—a vision of a hidden chamber known as the Chamber of Reflection.
It was said that within the chamber's heart, the power to acquire profound insights and reflect upon the truths of existence was hidden.

Intrigued by the vision, Parisa embarked on a quest to find the Chamber of Reflection. Guided by the faint whispers of scholarly voices and the scent of old parchment, she journeyed through corridors that seemed to hold the echoes of countless thoughts and manuscripts that carried an aura of intellectual resonance, embracing the path that the chamber's enigma promised.

After days of deciphering cryptic scripts and immersing herself in the world of ancient knowledge, Parisa arrived at a chamber where the Chamber of Reflection was said to reside—a sanctuary of wisdom and the connection between scholar and insight. In its centre stood the Chamber's Chalice—an ornate chalice adorned with symbols that seemed to reflect the dance of ideas and philosophies. Parisa approached the chalice, and as she did, the air seemed to vibrate with the resonance of deep contemplation.

With reverence, Parisa gazed into the chalice's depths, allowing her intellect to merge with the mysteries of existence. With each moment of reflection, she felt the currents of wisdom flowing through her consciousness, and her understanding of the world expanded. She pondered questions that transcended time and space, witnessed the chalice's surface reflecting profound truths, and realised that within the Chamber of Reflection, the boundaries between individual thoughts and universal insights were blurred—a testament to the interwoven dance of inquiry and enlightenment.

As candlelight flickered within the chamber and Parisa's contemplations deepened, her journey of seeking profound knowledge grew more profound. She encountered fellow scholars who shared their own perspectives on the nature of reality, engaged in discussions that celebrated the symbiotic relationship between inquiry and understanding, and observed the essence of universal truth woven into the very fabric of existence. She understood that the Chamber of Reflection was not just a location—it was a realm where scholars communed with the essence of wisdom.

With each enlightened thought, Parisa's heart swelled with a profound sense of unity. She knew that the Chamber of Reflection was not just a place—it was a space where insights merged with the cosmos. She realised that the bond between scholar and chalice was a dance of interconnected energies—a symphony of intellectual exploration and the pursuit of truth.

As the chamber's ambiance deepened and the chalice's symbols seemed to glow with inner brilliance, Parisa's experience gradually came to an end, leaving her before the Chalice bathed in a soft, otherworldly light.

She knew that the chalice had granted her a gift—the ability to reflect not only on her studies but on the very fabric of existence.

With gratitude in her heart, Parisa left the chamber and continued her scholarly pursuits, carrying with her the insights and revelations she had gained. She shared the tale of the "Chalice of Wisdom" and the wisdom of her intellectual journey with her fellow scholars and seekers of profound understanding, reminding them that the bond between scholar and chalice was a dance of interconnected energies, and that the pursuit of reflecting upon the truths of existence within the heart of a dedicated scholar's chamber was a symphony of unity and intellectual exploration.

And so, dear listener, the story of Parisa and the "Chalice of Wisdom" teaches us that enlightenment transcends the boundaries of individual thoughts, that the bond between scholar and chalice is a dance of interconnected energies, and that the essence of seeking profound insights within the heart of a scholar's chamber is a timeless truth from the heart of ancient Persia.

The Legacy of Ancient Persia's Tales

As the final embers of our journey through the tales of ancient Persia gently fade, we find ourselves returning to the present, enriched by the stories that have woven their magic around us. The tapestry of narratives, inspired by a land of kings and queens, scholars and poets, warriors and artisans, has offered us glimpses into a realm that once flourished beneath the sun-kissed skies.

These stories, culled from the annals of time and brought to life with words, hold within their essence the very spirit of ancient Persia. They remind us that the echoes of valorous deeds and profound wisdom continue to reverberate through the corridors of history, carrying the essence of a culture that shaped the world.

With each story, we have traversed bustling marketplaces, walked the halls of scholarly institutions, and wandered through the tranquil gardens where poets penned verses that would echo through ages. We have met heroes who faced trials with unwavering courage, thinkers who sought truth amid mysteries, and seekers who found solace in the enigmatic embrace of the stars.

Yet, beyond the tales themselves, there lies a greater truth—a testament to the enduring power of storytelling. Just as a skilled artisan weaves threads into a breathtaking tapestry, so too do these narratives bind us to a shared human experience. They transcend time, culture, and distance, connecting us with the hearts and minds of those who came before.

As we close the chapter on this collection of stories, let us carry their lessons and insights with us. Let us remember the courage, wisdom, and unity that defined ancient Persia, and may these echoes of the past guide us as we navigate the present and shape the future.

The legacy of ancient Persia's tales lives on, an everlasting source of inspiration and enchantment, ready to be discovered anew by generations yet to come. And so, as we bid farewell to this journey through time, may the spirit of these narratives continue to weave its magic, reminding us that the stories of the past are the foundation upon which the stories of our own lives are built.

Printed in Great Britain
by Amazon